Jesus left his followers with only one ... Olander and Mutuku provide disciple ... simple resource. Out of their convictic ... of transforming people and that we ... process", they present to the disciple m ... *how* each may engage in that role most effectively. Their genius is that they draw examples, lessons, and reflections out of their rich store of experience in doing discipleship in the African context, both as disciple makers themselves and as long-term trainers of disciple makers in this context. In the book, I reconnect with my personal discipler and mentor Mark and my co-worker Mutuku. I recommend this resource as the number one carry-on for pastors, ministry trainers, mentors, evangelists, lay leaders – for every believer who desires to obey Jesus's great commission confidently in the 21st century on this continent, and everywhere else.

—*Rev Mike M. Mutua, College Principal at Pwani International Christian College and Bishop of LifePoint Ministry Kenya*

This is an outstanding book on being and making disciples. It is quite comprehensive, very biblical, and reflects the authors' commitment to making biblical disciples. It covers the life and discipleship ministry of Jesus Christ and includes a good section on how to follow up a new believer. Each section has an important reflection task. The book makes an excellent classroom textbook. I hope that the book finds a very wide readership as the authors follow Jesus's command to go into all the world and make disciples.

—*Rev George Janvier, Distinguished Professor of Education at Jos ECWA Theological Seminary*

Being a Christian is not just about attending church, singing, listening to a good sermon, and praying. It involves daily and intentionally following Jesus. Church growth should not be confused with growth in numbers; it is about converts becoming disciples through daily following Jesus. *The Discipler's Toolkit* meets this need for discipleship for the Church in Africa. I wish I had read it when I began pastoral ministry about three decades ago. I recommend it for all serious African pastors.

—**Rev Kioko Mwangangi, Pastor in the Africa Inland Church**

A wonderful and timely reminder that God has the answers to every question. This is an antidote for discipleship frustrations. Enlightening and highly readable, The Discipler's Toolkit thoughtfully explores the mystery of divine wisdom and skills needed for world-class evangelistic exploits. This book is a compendium of resources for a stress-free soul-winning and discipleship adventure. The arrival of this book is a great news.

—**Pastor Felix Fahuwa, lead pastor of Kingdom Promises International Ministry, Lagos**

The Discipler's Toolkit deserves to be in the hands of every serious Christian and church leader in Africa. This well-researched and practical book is rooted in Scripture and covers the whole spectrum of discipleship. It is filled with African stories, diagrams, numerous suggestions of how to make disciples, and "stop and reflect" questions.

—**Dr Richard J. Gehman, former Principal of Scott Theological College**

In faithful obedience to Jesus's Great Commission, this book is an essential step-by-step guide that is easy to follow and adapt in disciple making. It awakens and fans a zeal for discipling and perfecting the skills for that vital ministry. The methods, illustrations, and examples presented in the book are clear and applicable everywhere on Earth, especially in Africa. I recommend it fully.

—**Rev Dr Nathan Nzyoka Joshua, Lecturer in Biblical Studies at Africa International University, Nairobi, Kenya**

25
TOOLS TO MULTIPLY
YOUR IMPACT

The
Discipler's
Toolkit

George M. Mutuku and Mark A. Olander

OASIS
INTERNATIONAL
PUBLISHING

The Discipler's Toolkit.
Copyright © 2022 by Mark A. Olander.

ISBN 13: 978-1-59452-815-6
ISBN: 1-59452-815-2

Published by Oasis International Ltd.

Oasis International is a ministry devoted to growing discipleship through publishing African voices.
- We *engage* Africa's most influential, most relevant, and best communicators for the sake of the gospel.
- We *cultivate* local and global partnerships in order to publish and distribute high-quality books and Bibles.
- We *create* contextual content that meets the specific needs of Africa, has the power to transform individuals and societies, and gives the church in Africa a global voice.

Oasis is: *Satisfying Africa's Thirst for God's Word.* For more information, go to oasisinternational.com.

Cover design: Soliu Akande.
Interior design: Lindie Nel.

Printed in India.

22 23 24 25 26 27 28 29 30 31 BPI 10 9 8 7 6 5 4 3 2 1

Table of Contents

To Ruth Mbithi and Jan Olander,
our loving and supportive wives
whose lives continually inspire us
to walk humbly with God
and to serve him wholeheartedly.

He has shown you, O mortal, what is good.
And what does the Lord require of you?
To act justly
and to love mercy
and to walk humbly with your God.
(Micah 6:8)

But be sure to fear the Lord
and serve him faithfully with all your heart;
consider what great things he has done for you.
(1 Samuel 12:24)

1

The Challenge before Us

THE NEED OF THE HOUR

For those of us who are Christians, it is exciting to see the unprecedented spread of Christianity in Africa these days. Particularly in sub-Saharan countries, the church of Jesus Christ is growing at an astonishing rate. Many local churches are overflowing with large numbers of worshippers on Sunday mornings and new churches are founded every day across the continent.

Even back in 1997, Tokunboh Adeyemo, who was a leading Christian theologian from Nigeria, made a reference to the amazing growth of the Christian church on this continent when he wrote:

> To crown it all, God has blessed and continues to bless Africa spiritually . . . Throughout the continent, with the exception of seven strongly Islamic nations, new churches are being established daily . . . Africa records an average of 4,000 new converts every day and this puts the Christian population in Africa at more than 50 per cent of the overall population.[1]

The *Africa Study Bible* editors suggest that one of the reasons for this rapid growth is a strong emphasis upon evangelism. They write:

The impressive growth of Christianity in Africa can be explained in part by Christians placing a strong emphasis on the Great Commission, which includes both evangelism and discipleship. Some say that African Christianity has grown wide but not deep. This reveals an emphasis on the first part, evangelism, but a failure to spend as much effort on the second part of making disciples by teaching people how to grow in their faith.[2]

Local churches in Africa are teeming with large congregations, but the Great Commission involves more than just numbers resulting from evangelism. Important questions to be considered are: "Have the members been firmly established in their faith?" and "Do they know *why* they believe *what* they believe?" Christ's command is to *make disciples*, not just to *win converts*.

Christian cults are also growing rapidly in Africa, and this is partially due to lack of biblical knowledge. How does this happen? If a person doesn't know what an authentic note of currency looks like, then he or she can easily be fooled by counterfeit currency. So it is with Christianity; new Christians need to be firmly established in their Christian faith so that they will not be misled by false teaching. It is one thing to ask people to make a decision to become a believer in Christ. And it is another thing altogether to help them become true disciples in the biblical sense of being fully committed followers of Jesus.

> **Local churches in Africa are teeming with large congregations, but the Great Commission involves more than just numbers.**

Therefore, pastors of local churches need to be intentional about making disciples who can spiritually multiply. Sadly, many local church pastors do not seem to see the need for disciple making. The result is that many of the Christians in the churches not only lack a *vision* for making disciples, but they also lack the *knowledge* of how to make disciples. If a local church fails to make disciples, then it is falling short of what Christ intends for the church to do. Spiritual multiplication should be a high priority for any local church.[3]

That spiritual multiplication is more than just evangelism was evident in the life of a young man named Yusufu.

> Yusufu was hungry. Not hungry for physical food but hungry for spiritual food. He went to his pastor and the pastor was too busy to disciple him. The pastor told him to come to church and Sunday school. Yusufu went to the elders but the elders did not know what to do. That is, they did not know how to train a leader. The elders finally gave Yusufu the advice to go to Bible school. Hopefully, he would receive training at school. Yusufu was surprised that no one in the church was able to help him develop as a disciple and leader.[4]

Why do so many pastors lack a vision for disciple making in their local churches? Possibly they do not see themselves as disciple makers but rather as church administrators and shepherds of the flock entrusted to their care. Writing in Nigeria, George Janvier describes the problem: "Traditionally, in Africa, the pastor is never seen as a disciple maker. [A pastor] simply preaches, performs ceremonies, and is there whenever people need him [or her]."[5]

Our mandate is clear. Christ has commanded us to give our lives to making disciples. Hudson Taylor, the well-known missionary to China, once said, "The Great Commission is not an option to be considered; it is a command to be obeyed."[6] This Great Commission that Jesus gave to his disciples prior to his return to heaven is applicable and relevant for Christians today. Zambian theologian Joe Kapolyo emphasizes this truth when he writes:

> The Great Commission is given by the highest authority in the universe, and it is binding on all disciples for all time. No other task comes with the same authority, the same universal scope or the same eternal consequences. To go

into the world and make disciples of all nations is the most exciting, most urgent and most necessary task in the world. As the number of Christians grows in Africa, let the church on the continent be found faithful in advancing the frontiers of mission for the honour and glory of Jesus Christ our Lord.[7]

The purpose of this book is to help equip Christians in Africa with the knowledge and skills needed to become disciple makers in and through the local church. This task of disciple making is absolutely critical because of the growth of Christianity and cults. Jesus gave his disciples the task of making disciples and they gave their lives helping to accomplish this mission. Jesus's humble band of disciples was made up of very common people (like us) whom God used to turn the world upside down with the gospel.

This is your ultimate toolkit to equip you with everything you need to get started making disciples. Just like there are tools like hoes which we use for working in our gardens and farms, there are a variety of tools we can use for equipping others in their walk with the Lord. We have studied the many books, methods, and resources for making disciples to create an essential toolkit for you in this book. We summarize the important insights of others and give real examples on how to apply these principles. We offer memorable illustrations and 25 of the resources we have found most useful in our years of making disciples. They are listed from A-Y with a bonus Z at the end!

As educators, we know that simply receiving information does not necessarily lead to transformation. However, when you stop, reflect, and engage with what you are learning, your learning is much more transformative. So we have also provided questions and spaces for you to write your answers throughout the book. Furthermore, it would be very beneficial to discuss your answers with others so you can gain additional insights from their perspective. Pause now to answer this first question.

STOP AND REFLECT:

Do you agree that disciple making is a weakness in many local churches today? Why or why not?

_____

_____

_____

_____

_____

_____

_____

_____

_____

_____

_____

THE GREAT COMMISSION

Before we begin to look at these tools, let's re-examine the Great Commission that Jesus gave his disciples so we can gain a better understanding of what he was saying. A closer look will help us gain valuable insights that can enable us to make application to our lives today.

After his resurrection from the dead and just prior to returning to his Father in heaven, Jesus gave his disciples clear instructions as to what he wanted them to do. In fact, he gave them a command. Each of the four Gospel writers records a slightly different rendering of this command given to his apostles (Matthew 28:18-20; Mark 16:15; Luke 24:46-47; John 20:21). In part two of Luke's writings, Acts 1:8, he records another instruction for Jesus's apostles to follow after he left them and returned to his Father in heaven.

However, the clearest and most comprehensive statement of what Christians refer to as the Great Commission is recorded by Matthew at the very end of his Gospel:

All authority in heaven and earth has been given to me. Therefore go and make disciples of all nations, baptising them in the name of the Father and of the Son and of the Holy Spirit, and teaching them to obey everything I have commanded you. And surely I am with you always, to the very end of the age (Matthew 28:18-20).

This commission has several key words that are worth careful examination.

Key Words in the Great Commission

As a person looks closely at this commission found in Matthew 28:18-20, it becomes evident that there are several key words and phrases that shed light on the command which Jesus gave to his disciples. The phrase "all authority" points out that Christ has the ultimate right to command his disciples to do whatever he wants them to do. This power has been given to him by the Father. And it is with this power that he is sending them out to accomplish the mission.

The primary verb, the command, in the Great Commission is to "make disciples". Christ was instructing them that they were not only to share the Good News (the gospel) with people and win converts but also to disciple them so they would become people who are totally committed to following Christ regardless of the cost (Luke 9:23). And the phrase "of all nations" implies that the gospel needs to be preached and disciples are to be made from every ethnic group (not just their own), every tribe, every language, and every nation (see Revelation 5:9). But how were they to accomplish this task? Jesus used three participles to describe how they could make disciples.

"Going" could be understood to mean wherever they went. (For example, tradition holds that Thomas took the gospel to India, John ended up in Patmos, and Peter went to Rome.) But it is often translated as "go", indicating that the disciples were to take the initiative to reach out to others and not to wait for others to come to them. Jesus's primary emphasis was probably that the disciples were to go where the lost were. Likewise, as Christians today, we are to *go* to non-Christians, not invite them to *come* to us. In other words, we are to be proactive, not reactive. We are to be *seeking* the lost, not *waiting* for them to come to us to be saved.

"Baptizing" was a way a new believer could make a public statement to others that he had decided to believe the gospel and become a Christ-follower. It was a symbolic demonstration of being raised from the dead into a new life in Christ. Since these baptisms were generally done in public places like a river or lake, the whole community was aware of the new convert's personal commitment to follow Jesus.

We are to be proactive, not reactive.

"Teaching" refers to instructing the new believers in what they were to obey using various methods of learning. What they were to be taught is explained in the phrase "to obey everything I have commanded you". In other words, Jesus told the disciples that new believers were to be instructed to obey everything he had taught them during the three years he discipled them. And one of the things he commanded them to do was to make disciples of all nations! As Steve Smith and Ying Kai point out in their book entitled *T4T: A Discipleship Re-Revolution*, "Every disciple is to learn how to obey Jesus's commands, including witnessing to others and then training these new believers to repeat the process."[8]

Jesus then assured his disciples of his continuing presence with them saying, "I am with you always." He made it clear that he would be with them to encourage them and enable them to accomplish the task.

STOP AND REFLECT:

How would you restate the Great Commission in your own words?

_____

_____

_____

_____

_____

_____

_____

_____

_____

_____

Definition of Key Terms

What is a "disciple"? The English word is a translation of the Greek word *mathetes* which means learner or follower (cf. Luke 14:26). Hence, the word used for disciple in the Swahili Bible is *mwanafunzi*, which literally means student.

A disciple is a person who has heard the gospel and has decided to follow Christ and his teachings. In a sense, a disciple is a person in process who eagerly wants to learn and apply what Jesus Christ teaches him or her.[9] Furthermore, a disciple is someone who walks with God in every area of his or her life.[10] The primary characteristic of a true disciple of Christ is a change seen in the person's character, growth that results in continuing transformation into Christlikeness.[11]

Adeyemo makes the following helpful observation about the characteristics of a true disciple:

> Faithful disciples are characterized by qualities such as abiding in Jesus's word, steadfast faith in him, loyalty to him, love for one another, walking in the light, bearing

fruit, and humble service to one another (John 8:31-36; 13:34-35). Discipleship also requires obedience to his commands (Luke 6:46), specifically the commands to love God and our neighbours and to make disciples of all nations (Matthew 22:37-39; 28:18-20).[12]

What, then, is "discipleship"? Simply defined, discipleship is the process of following Jesus and living as he lived. It is a life lived being conformed to the image of Christ. When the apostle Paul wrote to the Christians in Corinth, he described the transformational aspect of discipleship:

> And we all, who with unveiled faces contemplate the Lord's glory, are being transformed into his image with ever-increasing glory, which comes from the Lord, who is the Spirit (2 Corinthians 3:18).

Therefore, the term "disciple making" can be defined as the process of helping other Christians grow toward spiritual maturity. One might even think of it as spiritual reproduction. Just as we multiply and reproduce ourselves physically in the children born to us, passing on our traits to them, so we are called to multiply spiritually, passing on Jesus's traits to those who are newborn in Christ. The basic concept is that a true disciple will be involved in making other disciples of Jesus Christ. Dawson Trotman, the founder of the Navigators, makes this observation, "Every person who is born into God's family is to multiply" spiritually. Trotman further asserts that "every one of [God's] children ought to be a reproducer".[13]

The Main Thrust of the Great Commission

As we have seen, the primary emphasis of Jesus's commission to his disciples is to make disciples. Everything else in the Great Commission revolves around this fundamental command. Jesus used *matheteusate* in the aorist tense to indicate that "making disciples" is a command with force, urgency, and priority. If this command had been given in the present tense, which is the only other option in the *koine* Greek, the solemn nuance of urgency and priority would have been completely lost. In other words, making disciples is the urgent thing for you to do and you should make it your highest priority in life.

To a certain extent, to be a disciple maker is to mentor a fellow believer. Adeyemo says, "A modern equivalent to apprenticeship might be the relationship between mentors and protégés. Mentors are trusted counsellors who help their protégés discover, develop and use their abilities."[14]

In the next chapter we will take a closer look at how Jesus discipled the Twelve. From his example, we can learn many helpful disciple-making principles that will develop us into effective disciple makers.

STOP AND REFLECT:

What are some practical steps that a local church can take to help equip disciple makers? What can we do to help Christians become motivated to take these steps?

_____

_____

_____

_____

_____

_____

_____

_____

_____

_____

_____

_____

_____

_____

2
How Jesus Trained the Twelve

This chapter will explore *how* Jesus discipled his 12 apostles during his three years of public ministry. He had a clear objective and used a definite method to making disciples.

THE DISTINGUISHING MARKS OF A DISCIPLE

Before we look at Jesus's method of discipling these men, it is helpful for us to note what Jesus himself identified as the distinguishing marks of a disciple. There are many Scripture texts in which Jesus mentions characteristics of a disciple. Some of these are internal feelings and motivations, while some are external choices and actions.

In the interesting verses of Luke 14:25-27, 33, Jesus says true disciples have a love for Christ so strong that other loves seem like "hate" in comparison. They love Jesus more than anyone or anything else in their lives. And that love, according to John 13:34-35, extends to other people. True disciples of Jesus not only have a supreme love for God, but they love other people. Only God can enable us to love those who disappoint us, fail us, or are hard to get along with. That kind of love is a mark of a true disciple.

Jesus describes the heart of disciples as hearts of self-denial, ready to lose all for Christ, to give up personal ambitions and selfish agendas (Luke 9:23-24). Instead, disciples are characterized by abiding; they remain in Christ and in his word (John 15:5-8).

These internal characteristics of a disciple produce external fruit. This might be what Paul refers to as the fruit of the Spirit: "love, joy, peace, forebearance, kindness, goodness, faithfulness, gentleness and self-control" (Galatians 5:22-23). Or Jesus may be referring to the spiritual fruit of bringing others to Christ. True disciples are workers in Christ's harvest who share his passion for the lost (Matthew 9:36-38). They are not indifferent to the spiritual needs of those who don't know the Lord but they have a burden to reach them with the Good News of the gospel.

Holding to Christ's teachings as absolutely true and authoritative is another distinguishing mark of a disciple (John 8:31-32). Out of love for Jesus flows obedience to his commands (John 14:21). Jesus once asked, "Why do you call me 'Lord, Lord,' and do not do what I say?" (Luke 6:46). Our willingness to obey God's Word is an indication of whether we are truly Christ's disciple. True disciples bear spiritual fruit which is evident to all those around them.

TWO ETHIOPIAN DISCIPLES

Negussie Kumbi was born and raised in a small village in central Ethiopia, about five kilometres from the town of Wolisso. Negussie became a Christian during his teenage years and was eager to get a Bible of his own. After he memorized 200 Bible verses, he was awarded an Amharic Bible by a missionary! He hungrily read his Bible and received quality Christian teaching in his church and from his Christian friends. Negussie grew in his walk with Christ becoming a strong Christian with a solid witness among his friends and classmates at school.

After finishing his schooling, Negussie became a high school teacher. During this time, there was a Marxist government which sought to undermine the Christian faith of Ethiopians. It was illegal for teachers to speak to their students about Christianity.

One day, some students came to Negussie asking some questions about Christianity. He shared his Christian testimony with them and offered them Bibles so they could read about Jesus's life and ministry.

Hearing about this, a couple of teachers also went to Negussie to get Bibles. However, these teachers reported him to the authorities and he was arrested with the charge of "spreading a foreign religion". Negussie was put in jail, where he was ordered to renounce his Christian faith. Because he refused to recant, Negussie was severely tortured. He said, "I would rather die than deny my Lord."[15] Negussie spent nearly six years in prison because of this determination to maintain his Christian faith. He experienced first-hand the cost of discipleship.

Eventually released from prison, Negussie attended a Kenyan Bible college and received theological training equipping him to serve his church back in Ethiopia more effectively. Four years later, he graduated and prepared to return to his homeland. Unfortunately, just a few months after he and his family returned home to Ethiopia, he died of kidney failure due to thyroid complications.

Negussie was only 41 years old when he went to be with the Lord. But in his relatively short life he had impacted many lives in Ethiopia and Kenya. During the Marxist regime in Ethiopia, he also helped to organize underground cell groups which were made up of people from his church. The result was that the membership of the church grew at an amazing rate even during this time of persecution. Negussie was a genuine disciple maker wherever he went – whether he was a witnessing as a student, sharing Bibles as a teacher, pastoring a church, or refusing to deny Christ despite torture. For those of us who knew Negussie personally, we knew a man of great courage and faith.

STOP AND REFLECT:

How does the life and testimony of Negussie challenge you? Do you think you would be willing to endure the kind of suffering that he did?

_____

_____

_____

_____

_____

_____

_____

An Ethiopian woman named Astarke Aledala had a similar testimony. After her conversion to Christianity, she became actively involved with women's ministries and served as coordinator of the Theological Education by Extension (TEE) program in the area where she lived. For many years, Astarke suffered persecution because of her faith. In fact, she was imprisoned for four years during the Marxist Regime in Ethiopia.

One day as she was returning home after teaching a seminar for fellow believers, bandits approached. They killed her. She died with her Bible in her hand. She had given her life to discipling Christians. Although she lived only 30 years, she invested her life well in advancing the Kingdom of God in Africa. She was willing to experience the supreme cost of discipleship.[16]

These two examples show us a resolve to be a Christ follower, even if it means enduring suffering. Their stories help us visualize the cost of discipleship which Jesus spoke of: "Whoever wants to be my disciple must deny themselves and take up their cross daily and follow me" (Luke 9:23). Helen Roseveare showed great endurance as a medical missionary to the Democratic Republic of Congo in the 1950s-1970s. She explained how every disciple who follows the Greatest Commandment will incur a cost:

> To love the Lord my God with all my soul will involve a spiritual cost. I'll have to give Him my heart, and let Him love through it whom and how He wills, even if this seems at times to break my heart.

> To love the Lord my God with all my soul will involve a volitional and emotional cost. I'll have to give Him my will, my rights to decide and choose, and all my relationships, for Him to guide and control, even when I cannot understand His reasoning.

To love the Lord my God with all my mind will involve an intellectual cost. I must give Him my mind, my intelligence, my reasoning powers, and trust Him to work through them, even when He may appear to act in contradiction to common sense.

To love the Lord my God with all my strength will involve a physical cost. I must give Him my body to indwell, and through which to speak, whether He chooses health or sickness, by strength or weakness, and trust Him utterly with the outcome.[17]

While not every Christian will die for her or his faith, this is a good reminder that authentic disciples are not simply Sunday Christians. They are seven-day-a-week Christians who follow Christ, even when it involves great risk and difficulty.

STOP AND REFLECT:

What has it cost you so far to be a committed disciple of Christ?

_____

_____

_____

_____

_____

_____

_____

_____

_____

_____

_____

_____

THE THREE DIMENSIONS OF A DISCIPLE

Christ gave three dimensions to disciple making. These were the things he wanted his disciples to *know*, to *have*, and to *do*.

As we look carefully in the Gospels, we can see that there were certain things (truths) that he wanted his disciples to *know*. These truths included: his Father loves all people in the world; Jesus is God's Son and not merely a carpenter from Nazareth, nor a good rabbi, nor a faithful prophet; Jesus is the Messiah that the Old Testament prophets foretold would come to save humanity through his sacrificial death on the cross. More of these truths showed the disciples how to enter the Kingdom of God through trusting in Jesus and how to live in a way that pleases God.

There were also certain character qualities that Jesus wanted his disciples to *have*. These qualities included the following: a supreme love for God, a genuine love for people, an attitude of humility, a heart of compassion for others, a servant's heart, and an integrity in all aspects of life.

Finally, there were certain things he wanted them to be able to *do*. We can think of these as ministry skills they would need in order to fulfil their mission in life. These ministry skills included the ability to preach the gospel and share the Good News of salvation with non-believers, to make disciples of new believers, to minister to the physical and spiritual needs of others, and to effectively teach his Word to other believers.

We can see that Jesus had clear objectives when he discipled the Twelve. In the same way, Jesus has objectives as he works in our lives. Some are cognitive, some are about character, and some are behavioural. It is obvious that many aspects of our lives need to be changed if we are to truly be his disciples.

AREAS OF A DISCIPLE'S LIFE WHICH NEED TRANSFORMATION

The three dimensions listed above illustrate the transformation which was needed in the lives of Christ's disciples. Jesus had very raw material to work with when he initially selected the Twelve. But over the course of time, he was able to bring about a significant transformation in their lives.

In a similar way, as Christians today, we also need significant changes in our lives as we walk with Christ. Dietrich Bonhoeffer, a German pastor who was martyred for his faith during World War II, had this to say about the transformation that needs to take place in our lives:

> By being transformed into his image, we are enabled to model our lives on his. Now at last deeds are performed and life is lived in single-minded discipleship in the image of Christ and his words find unquestioning obedience. We pay no attention to our own lives or the new image which we bear, for then we should at once have forfeited it, since it is only to serve as a mirror for the image of Christ on whom our gaze is fixed. The disciple looks solely at his [or her] Master.[18]

In his excellent book on individual disciple making entitled *The Timothy Principle*, Roy Robertson points out that the ultimate aim of disciple making is spiritual transformation. It is God's intent to bring about radical change in the lives of his people. God is in the business of transforming lives. And we, as disciple makers, have a role to play in that process.[19]

God is in the business of transforming lives. And we, as disciple makers, have a role to play in that process.

Jesus saw many aspects and attitudes in the lives of his disciples that needed to be transformed. Our lives are being conformed to the likeness of God's Son. Paul points this out very clearly in his letter to the Christians in Corinth when he writes, "And we all, who with unveiled faces contemplate the Lord's glory, are being transformed into his image with ever-increasing glory, which comes from the Lord, who is the Spirit" (2 Corinthians 3:18). Our natural tendencies need to be changed into Christlikeness.

Bill Hull, a local church pastor, wrote a very helpful book entitled *The Complete Book of Discipleship*. Hull identifies six areas where transformation needs to take place in the life of a Christian. It was true of the men Jesus discipled, and it is equally true for each of us today. Here is a summary of what needs to be transformed in those six areas of our lives.

How We Think about Things

By nature, we humans tend to look at life from a human-centred perspective. We tend to put ourselves in the centre of the universe, acting as though the world revolves around us. God is certainly not the centre of our worldview. In fact, some non-Christians don't even believe God exists! I (Mark) remember the day when I was shocked to hear a fellow student of mine in a university make this heretical statement in class, "After all, isn't it true that God is a creation of humans, rather than humanity a creation of God?" Obviously, this student was a non-Christian and her radical statement reflected her human-centred worldview.

A human-centred worldview is also evidenced by prideful and self-centred thinking. The way we think about life in general can be very selfish. We need the Lord's help in reshaping our values to be consistent with the Beatitudes taught by Jesus in the Sermon on the Mount (Matthew 5–7). For example, we need to be transformed from being proud and selfish to being humble and unselfish. The apostle Paul exhorts us to be transformed by the renewing of our minds (Romans 12:2). This takes place as we study God's Word and understand better how he views life and wants us to think and live. Hull points out that as disciples we should desire to believe what Jesus believed so that we will be able to live the way he lived.

How We Live Our Lives

By nature, as humans we have a strong tendency to live a self-centred lifestyle. We tend to focus on our own agenda in life. We're looking out for number one (ourselves!).

But God wants to transform us into Christlikeness, which exemplifies a God-centred lifestyle. Living as Christ lived means putting God's plans ahead of our own. In Matthew 4, we read about the time when Jesus faced major temptations from Satan in the wilderness. His responses to those three temptations revealed his character.

The first temptation Jesus encountered was a test of whether his spiritual hunger would exceed his physical hunger. The second was a test of whether his character would triumph over his ego. And the final temptation was a test of whether his desire to worship his Father would triumph over his desire to control others. In each temptation, he gained the victory over Satan by using Scripture to respond to the deceitful enticements Satan brought before him.

How We Prepare Ourselves

Some of us thrive on routine and structure, but many of us have a human tendency to be lazy and to avoid self-discipline. We don't know about you, but we know for a fact that it goes against our nature to be disciplined. Like many, we want to take the easy way out and avoid it.

On the other hand, God is interested in transforming us into the image of Christ. We are, in a real sense, under construction by the Holy Spirit. When my wife and I (Mark) visited the Billy Graham Library in Charlotte, North Carolina, we found the grave of Billy Graham's wife, Ruth Bell Graham. The words engraved on her headstone are: "End of construction. Thank you for your patience." Apparently, this is what she requested be put on her headstone when they buried the "tent" of her body. She was aware that throughout her life here on earth she was "under construction" by the Holy Spirit. And when her physical life ended, the Lord took her home and the construction project was completed!

It is the Lord who is at work moulding us into the kind of people he wants us to be. But, at the same time, he encourages and expects us to be involved in spiritual disciplines which will help us become more Christlike. These disciplines include: fasting (Matthew 4:1-11), solitude (Mark 1:35), study (Luke 2:46-47), prayer

(Luke 6:12), worship (John 4:21-24), humility (Philippians 2:5-8), and sacrifice (Hebrews 10:9-10). Of the many books written on this topic, the two which we have found to be the most helpful are Richard Foster's *Celebration of Discipline*[20] and Dallas Willard's *The Spirit of the Disciplines*.[21] Reading these two books has greatly helped our understanding of the spiritual disciplines.

How We Relate to Others

By nature, we are inclined to look at relationships with a mindset of "What can I *get* from others?" When our selfish nature rears its ugly head, we recognize this tendency we all have.

But when we have a Christlike attitude, we will have the mindset of "What can I *give* to others?" Instead of thinking about how we can benefit from the relationship with others, we focus on how we can contribute to their needs. The apostle Paul wrote about this in his letter to the Philippian Christians saying they should imitate Christ, "not looking to your own interests but each of you to the interests of the others" (Philippians 2:4).

A Christlike attitude is characterized by love for God and for others. In his book entitled *The Mark of a Christian*, Francis Schaeffer states that the unique mark of a Christian is love. Schaeffer writes, "Love, and the unity it attests to, is the mark Christ gave Christians to wear before the world. Only with this mark may the world know that Christians are indeed Christians and that Jesus was sent by the Father."[22] Jesus spoke of this to his disciples saying, "A new command I give you: love one another. As I have loved you, so you must love one another. By this everyone will know that you are my disciples, if you love one another" (John 13:35).

How We Lead Others

When it comes to leadership, many of us have a natural tendency to lead others with an independent attitude, wanting those under our authority to be subservient to our every command. By nature, selfish ambitions motivate us when we are in positions of leadership. Selfish ambitions cause us to long for things for our own personal gain.[23]

In stark contrast to this selfishly motivated leadership style, Christlike leadership is servant-leadership in which the leader seeks the good of others. Jesus told his disciples that they would be different from the world's leaders who grasped for honour, "Whoever wants to become great among you must be your servant, and whoever wants to be first must be slave of all. For even the Son of Man did not come to be served, but to serve, and to give his life as a ransom for many" (Mark 10:43-45).

> **Christlike leadership is servant-leadership in which the leader seeks the good of others.**

Gottfried Osei-Mensah from Ghana addressed this concept of servant-leadership when he wrote:

> Jesus said, "I have set you an example that you should do as I have done for you. Very truly I tell you, no servant is greater than his master." (John 13:15,16). How we need to thank the Lord that he has not left us without an example, and that the same Spirit that dwelt in him also dwells in us. May we be daily assured of who we are: sons and daughters of the living God, freed from ourselves to give ourselves in humble, loving service to one another. This is the biblical challenge facing Christian leadership in Africa today.[24]

How We Serve Others

The sixth aspect of our lives which needs transformation is the way we serve others. Our natural tendency is to seek positions of honour in order to be served by others and to get recognition. In other words, the motives behind our desire to become leaders are ones of pride and competition. Bill Hull says that these "are basic elements in Satan's strategy".[25]

If we are to serve with a Christlike attitude, then we will do so with an attitude of humility and submission. We will desire to meet the needs of others through obedience and faithful service. Paul wrote about this Christlike attitude when he admonished the Christians of Philippi, "have the same mindset as Christ Jesus: who, being in very nature God, did not consider equality with God something to be used to his own advantage; rather, he made himself nothing by taking the very nature of a servant, being made in human likeness" (Philippians 2:5-7).

STOP AND REFLECT:

What are two ways that Christ has transformed you to be more Christlike in how you either think, live, prepare, relate, lead, or serve?

_____

_____

_____

_____

_____

_____

_____

_____

THE MEN JESUS CHOSE TO BE HIS DISCIPLES

People were Jesus's method of building the Kingdom of God. He could have used many other strategies, but he chose to invest his life in the lives of a small group of 12 men, whom he called his apostles. Luke describes Jesus choosing them:

> One of those days Jesus went out to a mountainside to pray, and spent the night praying to God. When morning came, he called his disciples to him and chose twelve of

them, whom he also designated apostles: Simon (whom he named Peter), his brother Andrew, James, John, Philip, Bartholomew, Matthew, Thomas, James son of Alphaeus, Simon who was called the Zealot, Judas son of James, and Judas Iscariot, who became a traitor (Luke 6:12-16).

Although we don't know a lot about these men, we do know something of their background. Here is some of what we know about them.

Simon Peter was a common fisherman living in Galilee. His hometown was probably Capernaum on the northern shores of the Sea of Galilee. He was apparently married because he had a mother-in-law (Matthew 8:14). He had at least one sibling, a brother by the name of Andrew who, like Peter, was a fisherman living in the Sea of Galilee area.

James and John were also fishermen and brothers, sons of a man named Zebedee.

Philip was a young, liberal Jew. After meeting Jesus, he went to find his friend named Nathanael to tell him about this teacher named Jesus of Nazareth (John 1:45). Nathanael, who was also known as Bartholomew, was initially very sceptical that any good thing could possibly come from Nazareth (John 1:46).

People were Jesus's method of building the Kingdom of God.

Matthew, sometimes referred to as Levi, was a tax collector by profession. He was the brother of James the Less. Being a tax collector, he was probably not the most popular person in town! Many people hated tax collectors because they generally were dishonest people who often overcharged their fellow citizens to make more money for themselves.

Thomas was also known as Didymus (John 20:24). He has been considered by many to be a "doubting Thomas" because of his statement after Jesus's resurrection: "Unless I see the nail marks in his hands and put my finger where the nails were, and put my hand into his side, I will not believe" (John 20:25).

James, distinguished from John's brother by the name James the Less or James the Younger, was the son of Alphaeus. He was from Capernaum.

Simon the Zealot was a member of a Jewish revolutionary group (the Zealots) which was violently opposed to Roman rule in Palestine. They looked for every opportunity to rebel against Roman authorities. It is worth noting that Jesus chose a Zealot who hated the Romans and a tax collector who worked with and for the Romans to be on his team. This must have led to some interesting political discussions in their team meetings!

Lastly, there were two men by the name of Judas. One Judas, the son of James (Luke 6:16), was also known as Thaddaeus (Matthew 10:3; Mark 3:18). The other was Judas Iscariot from the town of Kerioth, a small town a few miles south of Hebron in Judea. This makes him the only one of the Twelve that was not from Galilee. He must have been considered trustworthy by the other disciples because he was appointed to be the treasurer of the group. One might wonder why the disciples didn't choose Matthew who knew a lot about money because of his former profession. Perhaps they didn't trust Matthew due to his reputation as a dishonest tax collector.[26]

Robert Coleman, in his classic book entitled *The Master Plan of Evangelism*, describes the process of disciple making and gives the following insightful observation about this team of men who Jesus selected:

> What is more revealing about these men is that at first they do not impress us as being key men . . . By any standard of sophisticated culture then and now they would surely be considered as a rather ragged collection of souls. One might wonder how Jesus could ever use them. They were impulsive, temperamental, easily offended, and had all the prejudices of their environment. In short, these men selected by the Lord to be his assistants represented an average cross section of society in their day. Not the kind of group one would expect to win the world for Christ.[27]

HOW JESUS SHAPED THE TWELVE INTO COMMITTED DISCIPLES

As we have studied the life and ministry of Christ described by the four Gospel writers, we have identified 15 things Jesus did in the process of training his 12 apostles.

Some of the things he did were based in his relationship with them. We learn in Luke's Gospel that *he prayerfully selected them* by spending the entire night praying before he chose them to become his apostles (Luke 6:12-16). Once chosen, *he spent time with them*. One of the most important things Jesus did with the Twelve was to have them with him and to do things together (Mark 3:13-15). As the saying goes, "more is caught than taught." Jesus's relationship with them began and continued with prayer as *he prayed for them*. John 17:6-19 shows us how Jesus prayed for those he was discipling and training. He knew that God would have to do a special work in their hearts and lives.

Spending time together meant he could *teach them by example*. Jesus showed them what it means to be a servant-leader when he washed their feet during the Last Supper (John 13:2-17).

As Jesus spent time with his disciples *he responded to their questions*. In Matthew 18:1-9, 21-35 we see Jesus graciously answering the disciples' questions about who was greatest in the Kingdom of Heaven and how many times they should be willing to forgive others who sinned against them.

In the Gospels, we read of many situations in which Jesus was clearly frustrated and disappointed with the attitudes and actions of his disciples. Nevertheless, *he showed patience with them* and continued to train them. In one example, the disciples failed to understand and remember his miraculous power (Mark 8:14-21).

Jesus took them with him in ministry. One of the most effective ways of teaching others how to do ministry is to take them along with you when you are engaged in ministry. In Mark 5:1-20 we read that Jesus had his disciples with him when he healed the Gerasene demoniac. Taking advantage of the fact they were always with him, *he used teachable moments*. There was a time when Jesus was asked by James and John if they could sit at his right and left hand in glory. He recognized this as an appropriate time to teach his disciples about humility and servant-leadership (Mark 10:35-45).

Teachable moments can be challenging. In these stories we see how *he used hardships and difficult circumstances to teach his disciples valuable lessons*. In Matthew 17:14-21, Jesus taught his disciples about the importance of faith through an encounter with a demon-possessed son. Overtaken by a storm while crossing the Sea of Galilee, he demonstrated his power by calming the storm (Mark 4:35-41).

In a more traditional way, *he taught them verbally*. There were many occasions in which Jesus taught his disciples and other followers through sermons and parables (Mark 4:33-34; John 6:25-69). After he taught them, *he tested their comprehension of truth*. Occasionally Jesus would ask his disciples questions to assess how much they really understood. When Jesus was at Caesarea Philippi with his disciples, he asked them, "Who do you say I am?" (Matthew 16:13-20). As a teacher, I (Mark) like to think of this incident as Jesus's midterm examination for his disciples! At least Peter comprehended the truth that Jesus was more than a carpenter, rabbi, and prophet. Peter had come to know that Jesus was "the Messiah, the Son of the living God."

He rebuked and corrected them when necessary. There were times when Jesus needed to rebuke his disciples because they said or did things that were wrong. For example, in Mark 8:31-33, Jesus found it necessary to rebuke Peter for looking at things from a purely human perspective instead of from a godly perspective.

Having done many things to prepare them, *he sent them out to minister to others*. On different occasions, Jesus deployed his disciples on missions (Mark 6:6-13; Luke 10:1-16). He knew this was an effective learning experience for them. When the learning experiences presented challenges, *he used the problem-solving approach*. When he challenged the disciples to find a way to feed the 5,000, he was encouraging them to problem-solve (Matthew 14:13-21). And when they returned from their missions, *he debriefed their ministry experiences.* After Jesus's disciples returned from the assignments he had given them, he would spend time helping them evaluate the experiences and learn from them (Mark 6:30; Luke 10:17-20). He poured himself into shaping 12 ordinary men into his disciples.

Robert Coleman, in his classic book *The Master Plan of Evangelism* organizes this process of Jesus shaping his disciples in eight stages: selection, association, dedication, demonstration, expectations, delegation, observation, and reproduction. He makes an excellent point regarding Jesus's strategy about his mission here on earth. Coleman writes, "Though [Jesus] did what he could to help the multitudes, he had to devote himself primarily to a few men, rather than the masses, so that the masses could at last be saved. This was the genius of his strategy."[28]

STOP AND REFLECT:

Why do you think Jesus focused so much of his time on training the 12 disciples?

What other strategies could he have used? Do you think these strategies would have worked?

_____

_____

_____

_____

_____

_____

_____

_____

_____

_____

_____

_____

A. Watching Jesus's Method

Of course, we can read about how Jesus discipled people, but sometimes it is helpful to see it visually. There are many videos depicting Jesus that can inspire you in making disciples. We also recommend watching them with your disciples as an interesting way of teaching them about who Jesus is:

The Bible video covers some of the major events recorded in the Bible.

The Chosen is a film series containing several episodes about the life of Christ. These dramatic episodes reveal many useful insights into the lives of those to whom Jesus ministered.

The Jesus Film is a well-known movie that has been translated into over 1,500 languages and dialects, about the life and ministry of Jesus based on Luke's Gospel.

Magdalena is also about the life of Christ but from the perspective of Mary Magdalene.

Walking with Jesus is a video filmed in East Africa. The five short episodes show a pastor discipling others by using the congregational, small group, and individual approaches described in this book. When showing these videos, it is always good to follow them up with discussion time to help the viewers to grasp the full impact of the video.

From *The Discipler's Toolkit* | © Mark A. Olander | Published by Oasis International Ltd.

DISCIPLESHIP CONFIRMED BY LIFE AND BY DEATH

According to tradition, 10 of the 12 disciples died a martyr's death. Jesus's disciple-making process was so thorough that in the face of imprisonment, persecution, torture, and death they clung to their faith and their message. Their relentless commitment to the message of Christ is one of the strongest pieces of evidence for his bodily resurrection.

Simon Peter is the apostle we know the most about because of his ministry as one of the most influential leaders in the early church. Although he denied knowing the Lord on the night of his betrayal (Matthew 26:69-75), Peter was remorseful and repentant (unlike Judas Iscariot) and the Lord restored him to fellowship (John 21:15-19). Later, Peter was imprisoned by Herod for preaching about Jesus and then rescued by an angel (Acts 12:1-10). He wrote two New Testament books (1 Peter; 2 Peter). It is believed that Peter travelled as far as Great Britain as he preached the gospel. Apparently, Peter shared a lot of information about the life and ministry of Jesus with John Mark, who later wrote the Gospel of Mark. Most of what we believe about the subsequent ministry and death of each of the apostles is primarily based on church traditions, with little other evidence. These teach us that Peter ended up in Rome where he was reportedly crucified upside down, claiming that he was not worthy to be crucified in the same way that Jesus was.[29]

James, the son of Zebedee, became one of the primary leaders of the church in Jerusalem. One of the first of the apostles to die as a martyr for his faith, he was put to death by the sword of King Herod Agrippa I sometime around AD 44 Luke records James's death in Acts 12:2.[30]

John, the brother of James, also rose to a prominent position of leadership in the early church. Exiled on the Island of Patmos in the Aegean Sea, he wrote five of the New Testament books: the Gospel of John; the three letters we know as 1 John, 2 John, and

3 John; and the Book of Revelation. Later released from Patmos, he returned to Ephesus where he was the only apostle to die of old age.[31]

Andrew became a missionary in Greece, Asia Minor, and Scythia (a region in present day Russia just north of the Black Sea). He was crucified on an X-shaped cross instead of the cross upon which Christ was crucified. Today that type of a cross is known as "St Andrew's Cross".[32]

Philip became a missionary in Scythia and in Phrygia. He was stoned and crucified in the Phrygian city of Hierapolis.[33]

Bartholomew became a missionary in Asia Minor and Armenia where he was flayed alive and then crucified.[34]

Matthew, the former tax collector, became a missionary to Persia, Macedonia, Syria, Ethiopia, and Egypt. Authoring the Gospel of Matthew was probably his greatest contribution to the Christian movement. He was martyred for his faith in Egypt.[35]

Christians in India today believe there is substantial evidence that Thomas, the doubter, brought the Good News to their country. He was speared to death and buried in Mylapore, India.[36]

James, the son of Alphaeus, was arrested by Jews who opposed his message in Jerusalem. He was stoned for preaching Christ and buried in there.[37]

Thaddaeus, according to an early church historian Nicephorus Callistus, was a missionary in several places including Syria, Arabia, Mesopotamia, and Persia. Callistus also indicates that Thaddaeus died a martyr's death in Syria.[38]

Simon the Zealot became a missionary to North Africa and Britain, suffering martyrdom by crucifixion.[39]

The apostles never wavered despite horrendous suffering. Many people have used this to point out that the disciples did not make up the fact that Jesus rose from the dead, because they would not have lost their lives for a lie. The fact that the apostles never wavered from the truth also confirms that Jesus discipled them well and they held fast to all he taught them. They based their lives on the truth, and were ready to count the cost of discipleship.

STOP AND REFLECT:

Was the strategy that Jesus chose the best one in the long run? To what extent was it successful?

_____

_____

_____

_____

_____

_____

_____

_____

_____

_____

_____

_____

_____

_____

_____

_____

_____

_____

_____

_____

_____

_____

PART I.
THE FOUR SPIRITUAL GROWTH PHASES

An African story tells about a hunter who went out with his dog to see what he could catch. Sighting an antelope in the forest, the dog chased it and the hunter followed. Unable to catch the antelope, the dog was distracted by a dik-dik and began chasing it instead. But the dik-dik was also too fast for the dog. While the dog was pursuing it, he noticed a hare, and gave up chasing the dik-dik to run after it instead.

Running after the hare, the dog came across a rat. Hoping that he could at least catch the rat, the dog changed course, yet again, to pursue it. Unfortunately, the rat sought refuge in a hole. When his owner finally arrived, he found the dog lying next to the hole panting. Imagine the hunter's disappointment to discover that the dog, who had begun by chasing an antelope, ended up outrun by a rat!

The Lord gave us a mandate to make disciples. That is our antelope. Unfortunately, many of us have given up the chase and are running after secondary and peripheral delicacies. We have lost sight of the main task and have been sidetracked by trivial pursuits.

This chapter, and the following ones, will help us reclaim our primary mandate and stay on the right course. Making disciples must remain our most important mission in life. The temptation will always be there for us to focus on other good things and activities rather than pursuing our primary task of being disciple makers.

The disciple-making process can be divided into four phases. This chart of the spiritual growth and development process shows the four interrelated phases. Each phase is important and necessary in the process.

 # B. The Four Phases of Disciple Making

Phase 1	Phase 2	Phase 3	Phase 4
EVANGELIZING	**ESTABLISHING**	**EQUIPPING**	**ENGAGING**
Disciple maker witnesses through life and word, giving the gospel to unbeliever	Disciple maker grounds new believer in the basics of Christian life	Disciple maker equips believer in ministry skills and spiritual disciplines	Disciple maker helps disciple reach others and disciple them
GOAL: spiritual birth and new life	GOAL: stability and spiritual growth	GOAL: spiritual maturity	GOAL: disciple becomes disciple maker

From *The Discipler's Toolkit* | © Mark A. Olander | Published by Oasis International Ltd.

In Phase One (Evangelizing), the disciple maker shares the Good News of salvation through Christ with an unbeliever who eventually responds to the gospel message and becomes a Christian. This person experiences new birth as a result of his or her confession of sin and faith in Christ. In chapter three we will explore the topic of evangelism.

In Phase Two (Establishing), the disciple maker follows up with the new believer who is a spiritual infant. The new believer has many spiritual needs which the disciple maker helps meet. It is like spiritual parenting in which the disciple maker helps the newborn Christian in the basics of the Christian life. We'll discuss this phase of establishing in chapter four.

In Phase Three (Equipping), the disciple maker helps equip the believer to grow towards spiritual maturity. The disciple, who by this phase is a spiritual adolescent, is equipped with ministry skills and spiritual disciplines. Equipping will be our topic of interest in chapter five.

In Phase Four (Engaging), the disciple maker helps the believer, who is now a spiritual adult, to engage fully in reaching out to others with the gospel message. The ultimate goal is that the believer becomes a disciple maker too. In chapter six we will illustrate the engaging phase of disciple making.

3
Evangelizing

Sharing the Good News

Many years ago, a British teacher named Jonathan (not his real name) came to Africa to teach in a senior secondary school in South Sudan. Jonathan, who was not a Christian, had a very negative attitude towards believers. Sometimes he would publicly ridicule Christian teachers and students at the school where he taught. He questioned the very existence of God.

Although most believers on campus feared Jonathan and stayed clear of him as much as possible, there were two Christian teachers at the school who had a special burden for him. Praying that God would soften his hard heart, they hoped he would someday come to know Christ as his Saviour. As they looked for tangible ways to show Christian love to him, they sought to be his friends, showed kindness to him, and sometimes invited him to their home for a meal. Looking for common ground, they endeavoured to show a genuine interest in his life.

During the next several months, the Christian teachers both shared their personal testimonies with Jonathan, but he showed little interest, maintaining a negative attitude towards Christianity and Christians. At times, the teachers almost gave up because it seemed he would never respond to the gospel message.

Still, they kept praying for a breakthrough. Eventually they discovered that he loved to read but there was no library in town. They began loaning him their books, one at a time. *Mere Christianity* by C. S. Lewis was one of the books he borrowed. C. S. Lewis was a professor at Oxford University who became a Christian as an adult. In this book, he presents the gospel in a very convincing way and strongly defends the integrity of the Bible.

Early one Saturday morning, Jonathan knocked loudly on the door of his friends' home. Opening the door, the teacher saw Jonathan with a big smile on his face. Enthusiastically, he explained that the night before, while reading Lewis's book, he came under conviction that he was a hopeless sinner who desperately needed God's forgiveness. He told them that he had gotten down on his knees by his bed and confessed his sins to God. He had asked for God to forgive him, for Christ to come into his life and make him a new creation. He made a commitment to become a Jesus follower.

For the first time in his life, Jonathan had peace with God! He just couldn't wait to share this Good News with his Christian friends who had patiently prayed for him and shown Christ's love for him. Finally, after all these months of reaching out to Jonathan, they saw the fruit of their evangelism in the life of their friend. They rejoiced with Jonathan who was now a fellow believer. God used these two Christian teachers to reach Jonathan with the Good News of salvation through Christ. The result was a changed life. As Christians, we are called to evangelize so that the Good News of how we can have eternal life can be communicated to people like Jonathan who are in desperate need of a saviour.

STOP AND REFLECT:

What principles of evangelism can you learn from Jonathan's two friends?

_____

_____

_____

_____

_____

_____

_____

_____

_____

_____

_____

_____

_____

_____

_____

_____

_____

_____

_____

_____

_____

_____

WHAT IT MEANS TO EVANGELIZE

In the most basic sense, to evangelize is to share the Good News of salvation through faith in Christ. Bill Bright, a Christian leader who founded Campus Crusade for Christ (known as Life Ministries in English-speaking Africa), defined evangelizing as "simply sharing Christ in the power of the Holy Spirit and leaving the results to God".[40] Evangelism, thus described, is a process by which the gospel of Jesus Christ is presented in a way that non-Christians are able to understand and respond to the message.

The author of the Gospel of Luke and the Book of Acts recorded Jesus saying to his apostles, "You will receive power when the Holy Spirit comes on you; and you will be my witnesses in Jerusalem, and in all Judea and Samaria, and to the ends of the earth" (Acts 1:8).

Another Gospel writer, the apostle John, wrote, "We proclaim to you what we have seen and heard, so that you also may have fellowship with us. And our fellowship is with the Father and with his Son, Jesus Christ" (1 John 1:3).

OVERCOMING THE OBSTACLES

Even though we Christians know that we are to be actively sharing the gospel with non-believers, there are reasons why we are sometimes reluctant to do so. These obstacles hinder us from spreading the Good News. Let's look at several of them and consider ways we can overcome them.

1. *Fear of rejection and criticism*: "What if they don't like what I share with them? They might think I'm some kind of religious fanatic! And, besides, I might lose their friendship!"
   Response: While we may experience a negative reaction from those with whom we share the gospel, we need to focus upon what matters most. Is it more important for us to be liked by others or for them to hear the life-changing Good News about Jesus?

2. *Perception that others aren't interested*: "People are generally content with what they already have and they probably won't be interested in hearing what I have to tell them about Christ." *Response*: Bill Bright calls this "the biggest lie from the pit of hell". In my experience, I have found that most people really are interested if we communicate the gospel in an interesting and appropriate way.

3. *Feelings of inadequacy*: "I'm not qualified to preach to others. Others are much more skilled than I am." *Response*: You don't have to be a pastor or theologian to share the basics of the gospel message. If you know Jesus, then you are qualified!

4. *Lack of knowledge of how to share the gospel*: "I don't know how to explain the message of salvation to someone else." *Response*: The gospel message is really simple. We're the ones who make it complicated. There are several simple ways to effectively explain the Good News that we will explore together.

5. *Fear of being a hypocrite*: "What if they think I'm a hypocrite when I tell them that I'm a Christian and want them to become one?" *Response*: When non-Christians raise the objection of "too many hypocrites in the church" they may be trying to avoid their own responsibility. Each of us is accountable for our own life. You can affirm that you, like all believers, are a work in progress, no one in the church is perfect yet.

6. *Fear of not knowing enough about the Bible*: "What if they ask me questions that I can't answer? I haven't been to Bible school." *Response*: It isn't necessary for us to be great Bible scholars in order for us to tell others about Jesus. If they ask a question you don't know the answer to, just admit that you don't know it. Commend them for their good question and tell them you will find an answer and get back to them.

7. *Procrastination*: "This probably is not a good time to witness to this person. I'll talk to them about Christ some other time."

Response: The problem with this thinking is that there may not be another opportunity! It is a delay tactic of Satan to convince us that there will always be another chance.

8. *Lack of gifting*: "I don't have the spiritual gift of evangelism like some other Christians do."
   Response: While it is true that some Christians are more gifted at evangelism than others, nevertheless, we are all called to be ready and willing to tell others about our faith. Peter wrote, "Always be prepared to give an answer to everyone who asks you to give the reason for the hope that you have" (1 Peter 3:15).

9. *Living the gospel is enough*: "My life is a witness, so I don't really need to say anything. They'll see Christ in how I live."
   Response: It is not enough for non-Christians just to see the difference in *how* we live. They need to know *why* our lives are different. We need to tell them the message of salvation.

10. *Not really necessary*: "They are probably going to heaven anyway."
    Response: We can never make that assumption. It is very possible that they have never heard how a person can be assured of going to heaven. They need to hear the Good News!

11. *Unsuccessful in the past*: "I have tried sharing the gospel before but never succeeded."
    Response: Success in evangelism is not measured by the number of people who respond positively to the Good News. Successful evangelism is simply sharing the gospel clearly. The rest is up to God, not us.

12. *Lack of non-Christian friends*: "I don't know who I can share the gospel with since all of my friends are already Christians."
    Response: There are non-Christians all around most of us, in our neighbourhoods, schools, and workplaces. We need to be proactive in building friendships with them. Those who do live and work in Christian environments can intentionally make new contacts outside of our familiar contexts.

STOP AND REFLECT:

Which of the reasons given for not sharing the gospel seems the most common to you?

Which of those reasons can you personally identify with?

_____

_____

_____

_____

_____

_____

_____

_____

_____

_____

_____

_____

_____

_____

_____

_____

_____

_____

_____

_____

_____

_____

_____

_____

One Nigerian woman had good reason to fear telling other people about Jesus, yet her bold proclamation inspires us today. Deborah Adeyemi Ladeji's parents expected her to marry a priest of the local deity Orisaoko. Her father finally allowed her to marry a Christian man if she would keep worshipping Orisaoko, carrying a python around her neck, and making money for the family. If she stopped, she would die on the seventh day.

Successful evangelism is simply sharing the gospel clearly.

However, after visiting church with her husband, Deborah became a Christian. At the next Orisaoko festival, she publicly proclaimed her Christian faith and told her parents she would no longer worship Orisaoko. Although she became seriously ill on the seventh day, she refused to recant and survived.

Deborah grew through discipleship. She would evangelize idol worshippers during their festivals. Although she wasn't able to convert her brothers, she converted all their children as well as her own. She had a strong spiritual influence upon her granddaughter and grandson who are involved in Christian ministry today.[41]

STOP AND REFLECT:

How can we as Christians overcome the obstacle of fear when witnessing to our non-Christian friends?

_____

_____

_____

_____

_____

_____

_____

_____

TWO BASIC TYPES OF EVANGELISM

- **Proclamation evangelism** is *telling* the gospel to others whether through verbal or written communication. Christians can do this by sharing their personal testimonies or by presenting the gospel using a variety of evangelistic methods.

- **Affirmation evangelism** is *living* the gospel before others through a lifestyle which demonstrates what Christlike living looks like. Christians read the Bible, but non-Christians are more likely to read the lives of Christians they know.

Our tendency as Christians is to go to one extreme or the other. However, both types of evangelism are needed if our gospel message is to effectively impact those to whom we witness.

Jim Petersen has written an excellent book on this topic entitled *Evangelism as a Lifestyle*. In this book, the author emphasizes that our lives must back up our words. We can't simply *give* the gospel message; we also need to *live* it out for others to see.[42]

IMPORTANT PRINCIPLES OF EVANGELISM

So how do we accomplish the important responsibility of sharing the gospel with those around us who don't know the Lord? One of the best ways to answer that question is by looking at some biblical examples. From each example we can learn several basic principles or guidelines that help us know how to most effectively witness to others.

Jesus and the Samaritan Woman (John 4:1-30)

1. *Ask non-Christians to help you with a need you have.*
   Jesus asked the woman to give him water because he was thirsty (John 4:7).

2. *Reach out to people regardless of their race, nationality, or religion.* Our natural tendency is to share the Good News only with people like us (John 4:9).
3. *Be sensitive to their felt needs.* Jesus knew her real need was to be in a right relationship with God, but the need she felt was for water. He started with her physical need before moving to her spiritual need (John 4:17).

Philip and the Ethiopian Eunuch (Acts 8:26-39)

1. *Ask good probing questions.* Philip began his conversation with the Ethiopian by asking questions (Acts 8:30).
2. *Listen to their questions and concerns.* He then listened carefully to the Ethiopian's questions (Acts 8:31, 34).
3. *Use appropriate Scripture verses.* Beginning with the biblical passage that the Ethiopian was reading, Phillip explained the passage and then moved on to share more of the gospel message (Acts 8:32-33, 35).

Peter and the Roman Centurion (Acts 10:19-46)

1. *Be obedient to the Lord's leading.* Peter obeyed God's instruction and was willing to go to Cornelius's home (Acts 10:19-23). God will also direct you to others who need to hear the gospel. Obey and follow where he leads you.
2. *Show an attitude of humility as you engage in conversation with non-Christians.* Show respect for them (Acts 10:24-29).
3. *Share the basics of the gospel clearly.* Don't make things complicated. Simply communicate the facts of the Good News in a way that a non-Christian can understand (Acts 10:39-43).

Paul and the Greek Philosophers (Acts 17:16-34)

1. *Move from the known to the unknown.* Paul had been observant in noticing that the Athenians were religious people. He began speaking to them by referring to an altar in Athens which had the inscription, "TO AN UNKNOWN GOD" (Acts 17:22-23). Start where people are and gradually move to a clear presentation of the gospel.

2. *Use words that non-Christians can understand.* Paul was careful to communicate with the Athenians in vocabulary that they were familiar with (Acts 17:16-31). Avoid using religious or theological terms which might be confusing to unbelievers.

3. *Recognize that people will respond differently to the gospel message.* After Paul preached the gospel message about Jesus to the Athenian philosophers, his listeners responded in one of three ways: some mocked him, some wanted to think more about what he told them, and some accepted and believed his message (Acts 17:32-34). We, too, can expect similar types of responses. Some will respond positively, some will reject it outright, and some will need some time to think about it.

So what does it look like when we apply these evangelistic principles and guidelines in a real-life situation? Let me (Mark) answer that question by telling you about my friendship with a man named Joseph. I first met Joseph over a year ago at a sporting event in our town. Although he is from a different ethnic group than my own, I was eager to understand his cultural background so I could more effectively reach him with the gospel message.

Over the past several months, we have been meeting for lunch occasionally. During those times together, I have been able to learn a lot of things about his background, his family, his occupation, his interests, his challenges, and his church experiences. I have asked him questions to get to know him better and to show him that I have a genuine interest in his life. I have realized that he considers himself to be a Christian because he attends church once in a while, but he doesn't seem to have a personal relationship with Christ.

Joseph and I have become good friends and I have a burden to see him come to know Christ. Several months ago Joseph's wife died unexpectedly. I attended her funeral and was able to meet some of Joseph's family members. Since then, he has shared with me about how difficult it has been for him to adjust to the loss of his wife. This has led to discussions about life and death issues.

During one lunch meeting, I shared my story of how I became a Christian while I was a student in high school. About a month ago he told me he is confused by the fact that each world religion claims to have the way to achieve eternal life. I agreed with him that all religions made by humans talk about what a person needs to do to "qualify" for entrance into some type of heaven or paradise after they die physically. I told him that all of these religions teach that the only way to reach heaven is through doing good works.

As I thought about Joseph's confusion regarding world religions, I was reminded of a small book entitled *How Good Is Good Enough?* by Andy Stanley. So the next time we had lunch together I gave him a copy of the book and told him that, in this book, the author addresses the commonly accepted belief that good people go to heaven. Joseph eagerly accepted the book and agreed to read it. The next time we met, I asked if he had started reading the book. He had already finished! We discussed some of the main points of the book.

Then I explained to Joseph how Christianity is unique in that the Bible teaches we can never achieve eternal life through our own good works (Ephesians 2:8-9). Instead, the Bible makes it abundantly clear that Jesus came to earth to die for our sins so that through faith in him we can receive the gift of eternal life. I explained that eternal life is a gift to be *received* not a reward to be *earned*.

Joseph hasn't come to a saving knowledge of Christ yet, but I keep praying for him. I believe someday he will become a Christian and experience the abundant life that only Jesus can give us

(John 10:10). In the meantime, I continue to be his friend and show him how much I care about him and his eternal destiny.

EVANGELISM THAT IMPACTS YOUR WORLD

If we are to really impact our world for Christ, then our lives must show evidence of abundant living. When unbelievers see the fruit of the Spirit in our lives, in many cases they will be drawn to know more about Christianity. They will desire to have what we have. This kind of life functions as salt which makes people thirsty. Jesus said we are "the salt of the earth" (Matthew 5:13). An abundant life (full of joy and peace) can actually make non-Christians thirsty for God.

Studying and applying the Bible to our lives is what equips us to live an impactful life. Spending time in prayer and fellowshipping with other Christians results in the abundant life that will draw others to Christ.

> **Jesus said we are "the salt of the earth" (Matthew 5:13). An abundant life (full of joy and peace) can actually make non-Christians thirsty for God.**

But to have this kind of impact on unbelievers, we must live in close contact with them. This can come about through everyday opportunities which we have in ordinary relationships with people around us in our community, in our place of employment, with our family members, at our school, at our church – during all our regular activities in society. There are Christians who deliberately isolate themselves from non-Christians because of the fear of becoming "contaminated". They choose to spend time only with fellow Christians. Unfortunately, that kind of isolated living makes it nearly impossible for us to impact the world.

STOP AND REFLECT:

Make a list of 10 of your non-Christian friends that you can be praying for on a regular basis.

_____

_____

_____

_____

_____

_____

_____

_____

_____

_____

Some Christians believe that witnessing simply means living a Christian life before their non-Christian friends. They say, "I live the gospel. I let my life do my talking for me. I believe that my attitude, manner, and actions will cause people to see Jesus. After all, I'm not an evangelist."[43] The problem with this approach is that non-Christians won't necessarily know *why* we are different if we haven't told them that it is because of our relationship with Jesus Christ.

Telling them requires sharing the gospel message in a clear and effective way. It means being diligent in finding ways to make the Good News of Christ understandable to non-Christians. It means using words that unbelievers can really comprehend. Our responsibility is to clearly explain God's message of forgiveness and reconciliation. Jesus said we are to not only be salt in the world but also "the light of the world" (Matthew 5:14). One aspect of being light in the world is that of making the gospel message clear. Later in this chapter we'll talk about some of the many ways we can do this.

If we combine living an abundant life before unbelievers with a clear presentation of the gospel, our world will be impacted. The result will be our ability to lead others into a personal relationship with Jesus. We will have a significant life-changing influence upon the people with whom we come in contact.[44] Being intentional about living our daily life in a way that attracts non-believers to the gospel means we will be salt and light in the world.

WAYS OF SHARING THE GOSPEL MESSAGE

There are many ways we can communicate the gospel to non-believers. We have found that one of the most effective ways of sharing the gospel is by giving our personal testimony. (Resource S gives basic guidelines based on Paul's testimony before King Agrippa in Acts 26.) In Jonathan's story at the beginning of this chapter, two Christian teachers used this method to help him see his need for coming to know Christ.

Many other effective evangelism tools exist. Here are some ideas to get you started:

C. One Verse Method – John 3:16

Adapted from Bill Jones[45]

1. Write the words of John 3:16 across the top of the page.

   > For God so loved the world that he gave his one and only Son, that whoever believes in him shall not perish but have eternal life

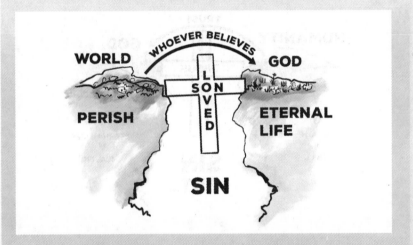

2. Label the parts of the diagram, as you write them on the drawing, in the following order: God, loved, world, sin, Son, whoever believes, perish, and eternal life.
3. As you write each word on the diagram, put a box around or underline the same word in the verse.
4. Ask them: "Show me where you are on the diagram. Have you crossed over from the world's side to God's?"
5. Offer to pray together if the person would like to commit his or her life to Christ.

D. One Verse Method – Romans 6:23

Adapted from Randy D. Raysbrook and Steve Walker[46]

1. Write the words of Romans 6:23 across the top of the page.

    For the wages of sin is death, but the gift of God is
    eternal life in Jesus Christ our Lord.

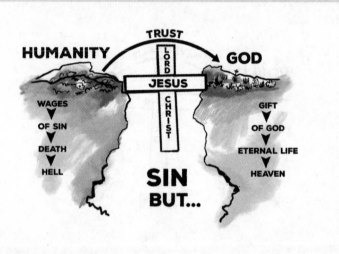

2. Label the parts of the drawing in the following order: God,
    humanity, wages, of sin, death, hell, sin, but . . ., gift, of God,
    eternal life, heaven, Lord, Jesus, Christ, and trust.
3. As you write each word on the diagram, put a box around or
    underline the same word in the verse.
4. Ask the person: "Have you crossed over from the world's side
    to God's? When?"
5. Offer to pray with the person if he or she would like to commit
    his or her life to Christ.

From *The Discipler's Toolkit* | © Mark A. Olander | Published by Oasis International Ltd.

E. The Bridge Illustration

1. Ask the individual, "Would you let me show you an illustration which shows the primary message of the Bible?"
2. See the diagram on the next page. Write the words *God* and *humanity* and explain that when God created humanity he desired for us to live a meaningful and abundant life.
3. Read John 10:10 and write *abundant life* on God's side.
4. Explain how we humans sin against God by disobeying him and choosing to go our own way. Read Romans 3:23 and write the word *sin* in the chasm between the two cliffs.
5. Read Romans 6:23 and write the words *spiritual death* on humanity's side.
6. Read together Ephesians 2:8-9 and explain that although people try to reach God by doing good works, they can never achieve it because eternal life is a gift to be received, not a reward to be earned. Write the words *good works* on planks extending from humanity's side but not reaching God's side.
7. Explain how God sent his only Son, Jesus, to die for our sins so that he could become the bridge to bring us into a right relationship with God. Read Romans 5:8 and draw a bridge in the form of a cross connecting the two sides. Then write *Jesus Christ* on the bridge.
8. Explain how we can cross the bridge to God by believing in Jesus and putting our faith completely in him. Read John 3:16 and write the word *believe* across the top of the bridge. Explain that to believe means to trust completely, to rely upon, to have faith in someone.
9. Review the entire illustration. Ask if the person has any questions about the drawing.
10. Give the person the pen, saying: "Show me where you are on the diagram. Have you crossed over from the world's side to God's? If so, when?"

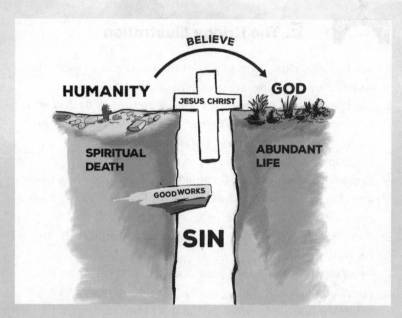

From *The Discipler's Toolkit* | © Mark A. Olander | Published by Oasis International Ltd.

 F. Bad News /
Good News Presentation

Adapted from Larry Moyer[47]

1. Ask the person if anyone has ever shown from the Bible how one can know for sure that one is going to heaven.
2. Tell the person that the Bible contains both bad news and good news. The bad news is something we need to know about ourselves. The good news is something we need to know about God.
3. Draw a line down the middle of the page to make two columns and label them *bad news* and *good news*.

4. First share the bad news:
    a. Bad News #1: We are all sinners (Romans 3:23). Share an illustration of how people who attempt to swim from the coast of Africa to the next continent will drown; in the same way, the gap between us and God is too big for us to cross in our own strength.
    b. Bad News #2: The penalty for our sin is death (Romans 6:23). Compare being fined for violating traffic laws to how we also owe a penalty for violating God's law.
5. Then share the good news:
    a. Good News #1: Christ died for you and me (Romans 5:8). Share an illustration of the person who entered a burning public transport vehicle to save the life of a child inside the vehicle.
    b. Good News #2: You and I can be saved through faith in Christ (Ephesians 2:8-9). Compare being saved to a rescue boat coming to save drowning people.
6. Ask, "Would you like to repent of your sin and transfer your faith from your own good works to Christ alone?" If so, offer to pray together.

THE BAD NEWS	THE GOOD NEWS
We are all sinners.	Christ died for you and me.
"For **all** have sinned and fall short of the glory of God." (Romans 3:23, emphasis added)	"But God demonstrates his own love for us in this: while we were still sinners, Christ **died** for us." (Romans 5:8, emphasis added)
The penalty for our sins is death.	You and I can be saved through faith in Christ.
"For the wages of sin is **death**, but the gift of God is eternal life in Christ Jesus our Lord." (Romans 6:23, emphasis added)	"For it is by grace you have been saved, through **faith** – and this is not from yourselves, it is the gift of God – not by works, so that no one can boast." (Ephesians 2:8-9, emphasis added)

From *The Discipler's Toolkit* | © Mark A. Olander | Published by Oasis International Ltd.

MORE EVANGELISM IDEAS

In addition to the resources above, you can use gospel tracts such as *Bridge to Life*, *The Four Spiritual Laws*, and *Steps to Peace with God*. You can also use evangelistic Bible studies such as the Navigator's *Rooted in Christ* or the Mailbox Club's *The New Life in Christ*.

Another method is street or mass evangelism. Billy Graham Crusades are a well-known example of this way of presenting the gospel message through evangelistic messages. In many African countries, Christians use street evangelism to present the gospel with a certain degree of success.

Christian literature such as magazines like *Today in Africa* also provide ways to share the gospel. While I (Mark) was living in Juba, Sudan, I met a young schoolteacher named Jino who had come to know Christ through reading an article in a Christian magazine. There are many excellent books like Josh McDowell's *More Than a Carpenter* and Frank Morrison's *Who Moved the Stone?* Jonathan, at the beginning of this chapter, understood the gospel after reading C. S. Lewis's *Mere Christianity*.

No matter what method of evangelism you use, you must enter into people's physical context to share your faith with them. For instance, you often meet people on the road or paths moving from one place to another. You can join them in their journey and as you go with them on the way, tell them about Jesus who is the way to the Father (John 14). In the village, you will find people tilling their farms. Rather than distracting them from their work, tell them about God who is the gardener working in us, because we are his field (John 15). If people near you spend a lot of time fetching water, this is a great opportunity to talk to them about Jesus who gives the water of life (John 4). Herders in your community may easily understand the image of God as our shepherd (Psalm 23).

In the country of Kenya, there is an area called the Kitui District. Historically, part of this area was evangelized by a man who came from farther north near the Mount Kenya region. He came to the area carrying sugar. He gave it the local people, who had never seen or tasted sugar before. The missionary asked them to taste it and they were amazed at how sweet it was. He then spoke of Jesus who he told them was sweeter than sugar. Many of them gave their lives to the Lord through this simple message. The missionary knew how to share the gospel in a way that people could easily understand.

Another creative evangelizer was Grace Zwane. After she became a Christian at age 29, she was burdened for non-believers. She used to witness to fellow passengers when she travelled on commuter trains in the Johannesburg area. She attended a Bible College at Siteki, joined the Moroka Church, and served in Soweto for many years. Her passion was to spread the gospel message wherever she went. She held revival meetings, led evangelistic campaigns, and invested in young people through youth camps and Vacation Bible Schools. As a result of her ministry of evangelism, countless fellow South Africans came to know Christ.[48]

This is by no means an exhaustive list of all the methods of evangelism. Let Grace Zwane and the missionary to Kitui inspire you to discover your own creative and effective ways to witness.

STOP AND REFLECT:

What is your greatest motivation for evangelizing and telling others about Jesus? How can we motivate and encourage other believers to share their faith with others?

_____

_____

_____

_____

_____

_____

_____

_____

4

Establishing

Following up New Believers

Matthew was a young man from Madagascar who had become a Christian at the age of 18 while he was in high school. Unfortunately, no one helped this young Christian become established in his faith. Matthew needed help in the basics of Christian life, but nobody in his church was willing to take time to disciple him. Church attendance was the extent of his spiritual nurturing. Simply hearing sermons on Sunday mornings was not adequate. As a result, his growth and development as a Christian was minimal.

Eight years later, Matthew earned a Fulbright Scholarship which enabled him to pursue a master's degree at a university in another country. Shortly after joining the university, he met a Christian who became his friend. Matthew was greatly encouraged and eventually asked his Christian friend if they could study the Bible together.

His friend was glad to do that. The two of them began meeting together weekly to study Scripture and share their lives with one another. Meeting regularly bonded them together. Initially, they used a Bible study book called *Growing in Christ* which covers topics like "Assurance of Salvation", "Assurance of Answered Prayer", "Assurance of Victory", "Assurance of Forgiveness", "Putting Christ First", and "God's Word". After they finished that book, they decided to keep meeting together regularly using other Bible study materials to guide their discussions. These Bible studies helped Matthew grow spiritually as he learned important truths about the Christian life. His relationship with his friend helped establish him in the faith.

STOP AND REFLECT:

What are some principles we can learn from Matthew's story of how a fellow Christian can help a new believer become established in their faith?

_____

_____

_____

_____

_____

_____

_____

_____

ESTABLISHING DEFINED

Perhaps the best way to think of establishing is to consider it to be spiritual parenting. Just as a newborn child needs the love and care of a mother and father,

Establishing is like spiritual parenting.

in a similar way, a new Christian needs the love, provision, and protection that an older, mature believer can provide.

One can describe establishing as _the process of helping a new believer to become established and grounded in the basics of the Christian life._ A disciple maker should be aware of the basic needs that every new Christian has and be intentional about helping to meet them.

BIBLICAL EXAMPLES

The Bible gives many examples of establishing. Barnabas followed up Saul (later known as Paul) after his conversion. Many believers were sceptical of Saul's conversion experience, but Barnabas stood up for him and nurtured him as a new believer (Acts 9:26-30; 11:25-26).

Paul and Barnabas illustrate another example when they planted churches on their first missionary journey and then returned to them later. The purpose of these visits was to find out how these new believers were doing spiritually (Acts 15:36-41).

A third biblical example is Paul taking a young man named Timothy under his wing spiritually (Acts 16:1-3). Letters were another way that Paul helped Timothy become established in his faith (1 Timothy 1:1-2; 2 Timothy 2:1-2).

THE PROVERB OF THE LION AND THE GAZELLE

An African proverb illustrates well one of the most critical needs of a new believer:

Every morning in Africa a gazelle wakes up and knows it must outrun the fastest lion or it will be killed. Every morning in Africa, a lion wakes up and knows it must outrun the slowest gazelle or it will starve to death. It doesn't matter whether you are a lion or a gazelle; when the sun comes up, you'd better be running.

Just as the gazelle is in danger of being attacked and killed by a lion, a new believer is in danger of attacks from the devil, whom the Bible describes as a lion looking for someone to devour (1 Peter 5:8). For that reason, the new believer needs to be established. As disciple makers, we play a vital role in that process.

COMMON NEEDS OF NEW BELIEVERS

A newborn baby has fundamental needs such as sleep, food, love, and security. Someone must care for them, helping to meet their basic needs. Some of the most important spiritual needs of a new Christian parallel the needs of a newborn baby. The new believer also needs to feel *love and acceptance* to know someone cares about their well-being. They need to be nourished with *spiritual food* (God's Word) to grow. And like an infant, they must be taught how to feed themselves on the Word of God. The new Christian learns better with *an example to follow*. This is one of the most important things a disciple maker can provide.

New believers need someone to provide *protection and security*, especially when the attacks of Satan come like a lion. This sense of security can be found in *fellowship with other believers*, which is vital for encouragement and edification (Hebrews 10:24-25). When the doubts, which are sure to come, arise, new Christians need *assurance of salvation* to know that they are truly children of God saved through faith in Jesus Christ.

Similarly, they need *assurance of forgiveness* when faced with the many temptations Satan will use to try to defeat them and get them to turn back. They need assurance that God will forgive individuals who sincerely confess their sins and ask for God's forgiveness (1 John 1:9).

STOP AND REFLECT:

Think back to when you first became a Christian. What do you remember being your greatest needs as a new believer?

Who was most helpful to you in meeting those needs? How did they help you?

_____

_____

_____

_____

_____

_____

_____

_____

_____

_____

_____

_____

_____

_____

_____

_____

_____

_____

_____

_____

_____

_____

_____

METHODS OF FOLLOW-UP

Following up with new believers means being available to do life with them. The disciple maker must be ready to wrestle through the circumstances of a new Christian's life and help him or her apply God's Word to them. The Bible gives examples of many methods for following up with new Christians.

Praying for them is essential. The apostle Paul gives us excellent models of how to pray for new believers in Ephesians 1:15-21 and 2 Thessalonians 1:11-12. Paul and Barnabas's primary reason for returning to the cities where they had ministered during the first journey was to *visit the new believers* and see how they were doing (Acts 15:36-41). If we are unable to do this, we can *send someone else to visit them*. Paul sent Timothy and Epaphroditus to Philippi to check up on the believers there (Philippians 2:19-30).

> **Following up with new believers means being available to do life with them.**

When visiting is not possible, *write to them*. Essentially all of Paul's letters, which make up 13 books of the New Testament, were written to new believers to encourage and strengthen them in the faith. Modern technology gives us the additional option to *call or text them*. Whether we use biblical methods like visiting and writing or modern methods like social media and messaging, it is essential that we follow up new Christians to establish their faith.

EXAMPLES OF KEY TOPICS

The resources in this book will help you cover several key topics with new Christians:

- How to live a productive Christian life (Resource G)
- How to get to know God's Word (Resource H)
- How to know God's will (Resource I)
- How to have a daily quiet Time (Resource J)
- How to pray (Resource K)
- How to share your testimony (Resource S)

G. The Chair Illustration

The chair illustration shows how to live a healthy and productive Christian life. As Christians we need to trust and obey our Lord Jesus Christ. We need to put our faith totally in him and depend upon him in all things.

The four legs of a chair show the four pillars we need to have a balanced Christian life. We need to: (1) read and study God's Word, (2) pray to God expressing our thanks and bringing our requests before him, (3) meet regularly with fellow Christians for times of fellowship and mutual encouragement, and (4) be active in sharing our faith with non-Christians that we know.

1. Tell them this illustration shows six basic aspects of the Christian life.
2. Draw a sketch of a chair.
3. Explain that Christ needs to be the centre of our lives. Read Galatians 2:20. *Write Jesus Christ on the seat.*
4. Explain that the back of the chair represents the Christian's responsibility to have faith in Christ and obey him. Write *Faith* and *Obedience* on the back of the chair. Read John 14:21 together.
5. Tell them there are four ways that help a Christian grow spiritually. Explain that we as Christians need to be active in these four areas to maintain a healthy and productive Christian life. The four legs of the chair illustrate these four ways:

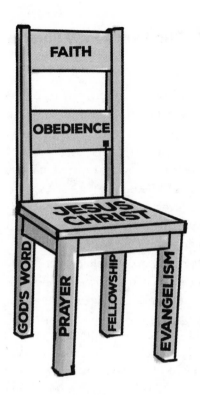

a. Write *God's Word* on the left leg and read
   2 Timothy 3:16-17.
b. Write *Prayer* on the next leg and read
   Philippians 4:6-7.
c. Write *Fellowship* on the next leg and read
   Hebrews 10:24-25.
d. Write *Evangelism* on the right leg and read
   Acts 1:8.

From *The Discipler's Toolkit* | © Mark A. Olander | Published by Oasis International Ltd.

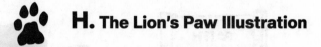

H. The Lion's Paw Illustration

The lion's paw illustration reminds us of ways we can enable God's Word to impact our lives. In 2 Timothy 3:16-17, we learn that God has given us his Word to: (1) instruct us as to how we should live, (2) rebuke us when we go astray, (3) correct us so we can get back on track, and (4) show us how we can stay on track in our spiritual journey as Christians.

God has not given us his Word simply to fill our heads with knowledge. Rather, he has given us his Word to change our lives. We need to be doers and not hearers only!

For God's Word to have its full impact upon our lives we need to hear it, read it, study it, memorize it, meditate upon it, and obey it. Only then will it change our lives.

1. Explain that this illustration shows us six ways that we, as Christians, can get to know and apply the Word of God.
2. Draw a sketch of a lion's paw on a blank piece of paper.
3. Label the parts of the lion's paw in the following order:
    a. *Hear God's Word*: listen to the Bible being read. Read Romans 10:17 together.
    b. *Read God's Word*: read the Bible (Daily Quiet Time). Read Revelation 1:3 together.
    c. *Study God's Word:* examine the Bible carefully. Read Acts 17:11 together.
    d. *Memorize God's Word:* commit Bible verses to memory. Read Psalm 119:9-11 together.
    e. *Meditate on God's Word:* think about the meaning of the Bible's message and how it applies to our lives. Read Joshua 1:8 together.
    f. *Obey God's Word:* do what the Bible instructs us to do. Read James 1:22 together.

I. The Hand of Guidance Illustration

As Christians we desire to know and do God's will. Sometimes it is relatively easy to know his will, but other times it is not as easy to discern. A genuine disciple wants the Lord's direction when facing decisions in life. The hand of guidance helps us remember five ways we can look for God's will. We need to ask him for wisdom and discernment, apply biblical principles, ask godly friends for their advice, consider circumstances, and be sensitive to our inner convictions. Following these five guidelines will help us know what God wants us to do as we make important decisions in our lives. When God is leading us, all five of these factors will point us in the right direction.

1. Explain that you would like to draw an illustration which shows five primary factors to consider when we are seeking to know the will of God.
2. Read Psalm 139:9-10 and point out that God promises to guide us by his hand.
3. Trace the outline of your hand on a piece of paper.
4. Label each of the fingers with the following words:
    a. *Prayer:* Read James 1:5 together.
       We need to ask God to give us wisdom.
    b. *God's Word:* Read Psalm 119:105 together.
       We should consider biblical principles.
    c. *Godly Counsel:* Read Proverbs 15:22 together. We should ask other Christians for their personal advice.

d. *Circumstances:* Read Acts 16:6-10 together. We should consider circumstances such as opportunities that open up and obstacles that block our direction.

e. *Inner Conviction:* Read Colossians 3:15 together. We need to recognize the difference between an inner conviction (which grows steadily over time) and our emotions (which go up and down).

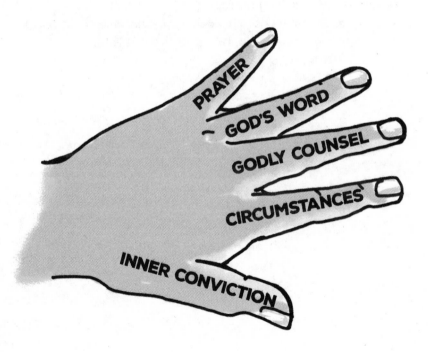

J. The Daily Quiet Time

Psalm 5:3 says, "In the morning, Lord, you hear my voice; in the morning I lay my requests before you and wait expectantly." This reminds us that we need to enjoy time alone with God on a daily basis. Here are some guidelines for how you can train a new believer in discipline.

1. What is a daily quiet time?
   It is an opportunity for us to spend time alone with the Lord so we can get to know him better by reading his Word and talking with him.
2. Why is a daily quiet time important?
   a. It enables us to deepen our relationship with God.
   b. Jesus often spent time alone with his Father (Mark 1:35).
   c. David regularly met with God (Psalm 5:1-3).
3. General guidelines to follow
   a. Find a place where you can be alone without distractions.
   b. Choose a time which is best for you (first thing in the morning, last thing at night, or some other time during the day).
   c. Bring a pen, notebook, and your Bible.
   d. Be realistic in your goals.
   e. Come with an attitude of expectancy (see David's attitude in Psalm 5:3).

4. How to have a daily quiet time
    a. *Ask* God for insight (Psalm 119:18).
    b. *Read* a passage of Scripture.
    c. *Examine* it carefully.
        i. Is there a *truth* for me to remember?
        ii. Is there an *example* for me to follow?
        iii. Is there a *command* for me to obey?
        iv. Is there an *action* for me to avoid?
        v. Is there a *promise* for me to claim?
        vi. Is there a *sin* for me to confess?
    d. *Write* down your observations and thoughts in a journal or notebook.
    e. *Respond* to God through prayer.
    f. *Share* what you have learned with a friend.

From *The Discipler's Toolkit* | © Mark A. Olander | Published by Oasis International Ltd.

K. Prayer Tools

Part of a daily quiet time is prayer. Many of us think of prayer as only asking God for help, but there are different parts of prayer that we often forget. You can teach your disciple to remember each of these parts of prayer using the acronyms ACTS and PRAYER.

1. Four aspects of prayer "ACTS"
    Adoration: praising God
    Confession: admitting our sins and asking for forgiveness
    Thanksgiving: expressing our appreciation
    Supplication: bringing our needs before him

2. What is prayer?
    Praising God for who he is
    Recognizing our dependency upon him
    Asking for his forgiveness
    Yielding our will to his will
    Expressing our thanks to him
    Requesting his help (regarding others' and our needs)

You might want to look at prayers in the Bible to see which of these elements they use and how they look. For instance, you can use the prayer Jesus taught his disciples (Matthew 6), Psalm 51, Psalm 102, 1 Chronicles 16, 2 Chronicles 6, Nehemiah 9, Habakkuk 1–3, Ephesians 3:14-19, or any other prayer you find in Scripture.

From *The Discipler's Toolkit* | © Mark A. Olander | Published by Oasis International Ltd.

CONCLUSION

No matter which of the many methods or materials available you use, it is crucial to establish new believers in their faith. It is our job as disciple makers to make sure they become, as the proverb illustrates, gazelles who are fast runners!

STOP AND REFLECT:

Do you know of a new believer that you could help become established in his or her faith? Write down that name. Ask God for guidance. Then, approach him or her offering your help.

_____

_____

_____

_____

_____

_____

_____

_____

_____

_____

_____

_____

_____

_____

_____

_____

_____

_____

_____

5
Equipping

Preparing Disciples for Ministry

A bright young Kenyan by the name of Mumo was accepted into a doctoral programme at a large university in another country. Shortly after arriving, he attended a free luncheon for international students and met David, who had once lived in Kenya. They had a good time together talking about Kenya and discovered they had many things in common. Over the next several weeks and months, a close friendship developed between them.

Sometime later, David asked if Mumo would be interested in meeting regularly to study the Bible and pray together. Mumo was eager to do so because he desired to mature as a Christian. He had become a Christian during his high school years in Kenya and attended a good church there, but had not been discipled by another Christian.

The two new friends met together regularly for about four years. They often met at a small restaurant near the university campus where they studied God's Word together and prayed for each other's needs. They also did fun things together like attending sports events at the university. Their friendship grew until they became like brothers. David invited Mumo to visit his church and later he began attending regularly.

They were involved in ministry together in various ways such as singing together in a small musical group called "The Jabulani Brothers". As one of the singers, Mumo was asked to give his personal testimony of coming to know Christ. Occasionally they spoke together at meetings attended by Christians from the Democratic Republic of Congo. While David taught in English, Mumo translated the lessons into Swahili so the Congolese could understand. As he was given multiple opportunities to develop and exercise Christian ministry skills, Mumo was being equipped to serve as a Christian leader for the rest of his life.

EQUIPPING: THINGS TO KNOW, BE, AND DO

Equipping is *the process of helping Christians grow toward spiritual maturity and develop necessary ministry skills.* It is when an older, more mature Christian seeks to help a younger believer grow in knowledge, character, and skills.

A mature disciple needs to grasp some fundamental knowledge about the Christian life. This includes basic doctrinal truths like sanctification, justification, and redemption. He needs to be able to use basic Bible study methods like those presented in Resources L-P, V, and W. The importance of disciple making and spiritual multiplication cannot be valued too much. Both require active involvement in the Great Commission. Each Christian needs to understand how God has shaped him or her to serve him.

STOP AND REFLECT:

In addition to the topics mentioned above, what are other important things that a disciple of Jesus needs to know?

_____

_____

_____

_____

_____

However, knowledge alone is not enough. As Christian educator Lois Semenye observes, "Knowledge that is not applied to real-life issues will not transform lives. While memorizing facts [Bible verses] is good, it is not enough. Learners need to be challenged to implement what they learn."[49]

Knowing should lead to being. The Christian must demonstrate the qualities that spring from maturity. The mature Christian should have qualities such as: humility instead of arrogance, love for God instead of apathy, and integrity instead of dishonesty. Maturity is marked by self-control, selflessness, and self-discipline. The mature Christian will be obedient to God and willing to serve others instead of being served.

STOP AND REFLECT:

What additional character qualities should a mature Christian demonstrate?

_____

_____

_____

_____

_____

_____

_____

_____

_____

_____

_____

_____

Knowing leads to being and being results in doing. Christian maturity is marked by the ability to share the gospel effectively and provide basic follow-up (disciple making) for a new Christian.

Among the mature Christian's skills should be the ability to counsel others with the Word of God, lead a Bible study group, and teach basic

Knowing should lead to being.

ministry skills and spiritual disciplines. Equipping is the process of training the new believer in these skills that will allow the disciple to become a disciple maker.

Of all these qualities, one of the most important is obedience to God and his Word. In his classic book entitled *The Training of the Twelve*, A. B. Bruce addresses the necessity of total obedience in the disciple. He writes,

> [Jesus would wish to see] every believer give himself up to [Christ's] will in cheerful, exact, habitual obedience, deeming all His orders wise, all His arrangements good, acknowledging His right to dispose of us as He pleases, content to serve Him in a little place or in a large one, by doing or by suffering, for a long period or a short, in life or by death, if only He be glorified.[50]

STOP AND REFLECT:

Based on your experience, what additional ministry skills should a mature Christian have?

_____

_____

_____

_____

_____

HOW TO HELP INDIVIDUALS LEARN A NEW MINISTRY SKILL OR SPIRITUAL DISCIPLINE

One of the most important responsibilities of a disciple maker is to help disciples learn new ministry skills and helpful spiritual disciplines. We've identified seven basic steps to follow in this process:

1. Tell them *what* it is.
2. Tell them *why* it is important to know how to do this.
3. Show them *how* to do it.
4. Do it *with* them, work together.
5. *Watch* them do it, observe, and provide constructive criticism.
6. Challenge them to *do it on their own* to gain experience.
7. *Reflect* with them on how it went so they can learn from the experience.

Let's see how this works out in practical experience. Suppose you are working with a young Christian lady and you want her to learn to have a consistent daily quiet time. How might you help her learn this important spiritual discipline?

The first thing you need to do is tell her *what* it is, to explain to her that a quiet time is when a Christian meets alone with God to read the Bible and talk with God. Then, help her see *why* the discipline of a quiet time is valuable and even essential for us as Christians to grow in our walk with the Lord. Use the image of the Bible as our spiritual food. Thirdly, explain to her the basic guidelines for *how* to have a quiet time, using Resource J.

The fourth step is meeting together one morning and having a quiet time *with her* following the guidelines you have explained. You should *lead her* during this time in the Word and prayer together. When she becomes comfortable with that, ask her to lead. You can *watch*, observing how she does and offering any suggestions you might have.

The sixth step is to challenge her to have a quiet time *on her own* for several days (e.g., one week) so she can gain experience doing it by herself. Finally, meet together and discuss with her how it went when she had a daily quiet time by herself. Ask her to *reflect* upon what it was like for her to have a consistent quiet time for several days. Lastly, encourage her to make this spiritual discipline a life-long habit.

L. Narrative Bible Study

This Bible study method and the four that follow it are adapted from *The Navigator Bible Studies Handbook*.[51] The narrative Bible study method is one that you can use with any portion of Scripture that is a record or description of events that took place in biblical history. Examples of this part of the Bible include the historical books of the Old Testament, the four Gospels, and the Book of Acts. To do this kind of study you simply need to answer the eight questions listed below.

Passage_____ Date_____

1. Where did this take place?
2. When did this happen?
3. Who was there?
4. What important thing happened?
5. What is the key verse of the passage?
6. What does this passage teach us about God?
7. What do I not understand?
8. What did I learn that I should do?

M. Verse Analysis Bible Study

The verse analysis method of Bible study can be used with any verse in Scripture. It is particularly useful when studying key verses in God's Word. There are five parts to this kind of study. The instructions are self-explanatory.

Reference_____ Date_____

1. Verse
   Copy the verse from the Bible.
2. Message
   Write in your own words what the verse says.
3. Context
   Record your thoughts and observations from the verses before and after.
4. Questions
   Ask and answer questions about the verse.
5. Application
   Write one specific way you can or need to change your attitudes and/or actions.

ABC

N. ABC Bible Study

The ABC method of Bible study can be used with any passage in the Bible. The portion of Scripture you study can range anywhere from a few verses to an entire chapter.

Biblical Passage_____ Date_____

A title
Give an appropriate title for the passage.

Basic passage
Write the key verse(s) which includes the central message of the text.

Challenge

      a. Verse of the Challenge
          Write the verse out, copied from the Bible.
      b. Truth of the Challenge
          State the truth of the verse *in your own words*.
      c. Personal Application of the Challenge
          Explain how this challenge applies to your own life.

Difficulties
Write out any questions or problems that this passage raises in your mind. Answer each question as well as you can based on your study of the passage.

Essence
Outline the contents of the passage or write a summary of what the passage is about.

From *The Discipler's Toolkit* | © Mark A. Olander | Published by Oasis International Ltd.

O. Topical Bible Study

Sometimes you may want to do a study on a particular topic like tithing, witnessing, fellowship, friendship, spiritual gifts, encouragement, or discipleship. The topical Bible study method guides you along as you explore the topic you have chosen. This type of study will help you understand the topic better and enable you to come to your own conclusions about what God says on the subject.

Topic _____ Date _____

1. Choose a topic of personal interest.
2. List questions about the topic.
   Write out some questions you have about the topic.
3. Locate Scripture texts dealing with the topic.
   List references and briefly describe the content.
4. Summarize what you have discovered.
   Either write a two-paragraph summary or outline the main points.
5. Select a key verse.
   Write out the verse and explain why you have chosen this particular verse.
6. Collect illustrations.
   Select contemporary illustrations as well as others from biblical or extra-biblical history.
7. Write out a personal application for your own life.

From *The Discipler's Toolkit* | © Mark A. Olander | Published by Oasis International Ltd.

P. Bible Character Study

Certain characters in the Bible may be of special interest to you. One of the most interesting ways to study an individual mentioned in the Bible is to do a Bible character study. Through this method you will be able to find out about the person's background, his or her strengths and weaknesses, and lessons we can learn from this person's life.

Bible Character _____ Date_____

Name of the person
Select a biblical person you would like to study.

1. Scripture references
   List biblical references with a summary of what you learn about the person from each passage.
2. Biographical sketch
   Write a summary of the person's life including the following: the meaning of the person's name, this person's background, influences upon his or her life, major events in this person's life, and his or her influence upon history or the lives of others.
3. Key verse
   Select a verse which seems to speak of this person's most noteworthy characteristic or quality. Write out the verse and explain why you selected it.
4. Character analysis
   List this person's strengths and weaknesses.
5. Leading lessons
   List several lessons we can learn from the life of this person.
6. Personal application
   Write out a specific application for your own life.

From *The Discipler's Toolkit* | © Mark A. Olander | Published by Oasis International Ltd.

Q. Bible Study Guides

In addition to the Bible study methods above, you can equip disciples using Bible study materials. We have found these helpful:

- Mailbox Club International (online studies for all ages).

- *Ten Basic Steps toward Christian Maturity* (Life Ministry, Kenya).

- *Rooted in Christ* (Navigators, Kenya).

- *Growing in Discipleship* (Navigators, Kenya).

- *Discipleship* (Evangelical Church in Zambia).

- *Christian Basics Bible Studies* (InterVarsity Press, England).

- Christian literature (books, pamphlets, journal articles), audio/visual materials, and Christian seminars and conferences.

STOP AND REFLECT:

Which of these Bible study methods is the most familiar to you? Which one would you like to try next?

_____

_____

_____

_____

_____

_____

_____

_____

_____

_____

_____

_____

_____

_____

CONCLUSION

As disciple makers, we rejoice when new believers are established in the Christian faith and equipped for life and ministry. This prepares them for the final phase of helping disciples fully engage, which we will consider in our next chapter.

6
Engaging

Getting Disciples Involved

Mustafa grew up in a strong Muslim home in a West African country. His father, hoping that his son would someday become an Imam, sent Mustafa to excellent Muslim schools for his high school education. After he completed high school, Mustafa told his father he wanted to study medicine and become a doctor. Although his father was not pleased with this idea, he eventually agreed to let him travel to America and begin a pre-medicine programme at a university there.

Mustafa was a very good football (soccer) player, so he joined the university team. One of Mustafa's teammates became his good friend. John was a Christian and Mustafa was impressed with the genuine interest his teammate showed in his life. Hoping to win his friend over to Islam, Mustafa invited him to attend his mosque one Friday. John agreed and was even willing to go a second time. Later, John invited him to attend his church on a Sunday morning. Mustafa was reluctant to do so, but he eventually agreed. He was surprised at the enthusiasm with which the people in the congregation sang and he agreed to attend a second time.

John shared the story of how he had come to know God through a personal relationship with Jesus and gave Mustafa a Bible to read so he could learn more about Jesus. Although he wasn't eager to read the Bible at first, eventually Mustafa began reading it. He came to believe that Jesus was God's Son, not just another prophet like Moses or Mohammed. He accepted Jesus as his personal Saviour and became a new creation in Christ! His life changed radically, and he began to grow as a follower of Jesus.

Over the next several years, Mustafa was discipled by fellow Christians and matured in his faith. He learned many helpful things such as how to share his testimony, how to study his Bible, how to witness to others, and how to serve motivated by God's love. Encouraged by others, he joined a local church where he met believers who helped him grow spiritually. Later, he became the teacher of an adult Bible class at his church.

Mustafa was challenged by his Christian friends to become involved in reaching others with the Good News of salvation through Christ. They taught him ministry skills like how to explain the gospel to others, how to share his personal testimony, and how to make disciples. Equipped by his friends, Mustafa began to reach out to those around him. After he graduated from the university, he developed a strong desire to reach fellow students who had come from other countries to study in American universities. His own experiences as an international student made it easy for him to relate to them. Mustafa became engaged in a ministry of evangelism and discipleship among international students at a large state university in the city where he lived.

STOP AND REFLECT:

What did fellow Christians do to help Mustafa become engaged in Christian ministry as a disciple maker?

_____

_____

_____

_____

_____

_____

ENGAGING DEFINED

When we see the term *engage* most of us think of marriage! However, here we are using the term in the sense of putting a car into gear. When we drive a car with a manual transmission, we have to push in the clutch pedal, then shift the car into the desired gear. As the clutch is released, the car is engaged in the selected gear. This action enables the car to move forward or backward.

In the spiritual realm, engaging means activating a Christian's involvement in serving and ministering to other people and making disciples. Dawson Trotman, the founder of the Navigators, addressed this need for disciples to be engaged in Christian ministry and disciple making in his interviews with missionary candidates. He asked them these penetrating questions: "How is your devotional life? Do you feel your devotional life is what the Lord would have it to be? How many persons do you know by name today who were won to Christ by you and are living for Him?"[52] These questions certainly apply to missionaries and prospective missionaries, but they also apply to all of God's children.

BIBLICAL EXAMPLES OF ENGAGING

The Bible gives us many examples of engaging, of which we have listed a few:

- Jesus sent out the 12 disciples (Mark 6:7-13).

- He sent out his 72 followers (Luke 10:1-12, 17-20).

- The Antioch church sent out Barnabas and Saul on their first missionary journey (Acts 13:1-3).

- They sent Paul and Silas to Syria and Cilicia (Acts 15:40-41).

- They sent Barnabas and John Mark to Cyprus (Acts 15:35-39).

- Paul sent Timothy and Epaphroditus to Philippi (Philippians 2:19-30).

WHERE SHOULD WE SEND THEM?

> But you will receive power when the Holy Spirit comes on you; and you will be my witnesses in Jerusalem, and in all Judea and Samaria, and to the ends of the earth (Acts 1:8).

Acts 1:8 gives us some general guidance as to where Jesus wanted his disciples to be his witnesses. Notice he named four locations. First, he talked about *Jerusalem* where they happened to be at the time. They were among fellow Jews, yet they would encounter persecution and opposition there. Nevertheless, Jesus wanted them to understand that they should begin where they were.

STOP AND REFLECT:

Where is your "Jerusalem"? Are you fully engaged in being a faithful witness where you live and work?

_____

_____

_____

_____

_____

_____

_____

_____

_____

_____

_____

_____

_____

_____

Then Jesus mentioned *Judea*, the area surrounding their immediate environment. In other words, he wanted his disciples to be willing to go beyond their immediate surroundings into nearby areas which might not be as familiar to them. Moving from the known to the unknown is never easy. You have probably experienced this in your own life.

STOP AND REFLECT:

Where is your "Judea"? Are you reaching out beyond where you are to witness to people who live beyond your comfort zone?

_____

_____

_____

_____

_____

_____

_____

_____

_____

_____

Jesus then spoke about *Samaria* which was a very different geographical area to the north of Judea. People lived there who were seen as inferior and undesirable in the eyes of the Jewish people in Judea. The Samaritans were descendants of Jews who had intermarried with Gentiles; thus, they were not full-blooded Jewish people. In fact, the Jews often despised Samaritans and wouldn't associate with them. Sometimes Jews traveling north from Judea to Galilee would cross the Jordan River and travel north on the eastern side in order to avoid going through Samaria.

STOP AND REFLECT:

Where is your "Samaria"? Who do your people consider to be second-class citizens or inferior people? Are you willing to share the Good News of salvation with people that you might have a tendency to look down upon?

_____

_____

_____

_____

_____

_____

_____

_____

_____

_____

_____

_____

Finally, Jesus mentioned *the ends of the earth* which represents the entire world. In other words, Jesus wanted his disciples to be willing to take the gospel message anywhere that he might send them. As we noted in chapter two of this book, traditional sources tell of many of the 11 disciples traveling to remote places in other countries to preach the gospel and make disciples.

The application for us as disciples of Jesus is that we should be witnesses and disciple makers wherever he sends us. We should also motivate and encourage those **We have to lead by example.** we disciple to do the same. The answer to the question, "Where should we send those individuals we have discipled?" is found in Acts 1:8. If we as disciple makers are challenging others to go anywhere the Lord sends them, we must be willing to do the same. We have to lead by example.

STOP AND REFLECT:

Where are the ends of the earth for you? It may be a foreign country or some other location within your own country where you might feel like an alien or stranger. Are you willing to go there if the Lord leads you to do so?

_____

_____

_____

_____

_____

_____

_____

A Scottish missionary named James Gilmour was once asked why he went to serve as a missionary in Mongolia. His response was, "I thought it reasonable that I should seek work where the work was the most abundant and the workers fewest."[53] David Livingstone, who spent the majority of his life as an explorer, philanthropist, and medical missionary in Africa, said, "If a commission by an earthly king is considered an honour, how can a commission by a heavenly King be considered a sacrifice?"[54]

In the film *The Distant Boat*, Maxwell Kioko, a young Nairobi businessman, experiences God's calling on his life to be a missionary to Muslims on the Kenyan Coast. In this fictional representation of a commissioning service, we hear the emotions of a young middle-class man who has struggled but obeyed, despite his misgivings about the area to which God has called him. He challenges his fellow church members saying, "Every sincere Christian must be involved in missions. Not everyone has to go, but everyone has to be involved. We need to take action. We need to give. We need to go. We need to send people. We need to finish the task." We love this movie because it helps us envision how Africans who respond to God's call can accomplish the Great Commission.

THE PARABLE OF THE RELUCTANT DISCIPLE

In the country of Mozambique, there was a Christian young man, Adelino, who was fortunate to have been discipled by other Christians in his local church. He even attended a few Christian conferences where he learned many helpful things about how a Christian should live. Adelino regularly attended the worship service at a local church and joined a small Bible study group. The only problem was that he never got involved in the lives of other people. He focused only upon his own life.

Eventually, Adelino joined his local church but didn't serve in any capacity. He had plenty of knowledge, but he didn't see the need nor have the desire to evangelize or disciple others. Adelino was becoming spiritually fat because of all the knowledge he was gaining. But he wasn't becoming spiritually strong because he wasn't exercising spiritually. Disciple making was something he chose not to participate in.

One of the reasons Adelino never became involved in Christian ministry was that he felt inadequate to do so. He didn't believe he had any spiritual gifts that could enable him to minister to others. In other words, he was like a spectator and not a participant. He was saved and discipled but not engaged in any form of ministry as a disciple.

STOP AND REFLECT:

If you were one of the young man's friends in the parable of the reluctant disciple, what are some things you might do to help him become involved in Christian ministry?

_____

_____

_____

_____

_____

_____

_____

R. Your SHAPE

When we hear Adelino's story, we can see that it is important to help your disciple discern where God is calling him or her to engage by looking at what opportunities and skills God has already given him or her. When God created us, he equipped each of us with a unique combination of spiritual gifts and natural abilities. Therefore, each of us is a unique individual created in the image of God. Because God has different tasks he wants us to do in our lifetime, he equips us with everything we need to accomplish those assignments. This combination of capabilities can be referred to as your SHAPE, and you can consider each part of your SHAPE as you discern how God may be calling you to engage.[55] SHAPE stands for:

1. **S**piritual gifts

   Your spiritual gifts have been given to you, not for your own benefit, but primarily for the benefit of other people. In the same way, other people have been given gifts for your benefit.[56] Some examples of spiritual gifts include: prophesying, serving, teaching, encouraging, contributing to the needs of others, leading, and showing mercy (Romans 12:3-8; 1 Corinthians 12).

2. **H**eart

   Your heart represents your desires, ambitions, dreams, passions, hopes, interests, and affections. Your heart represents the source of all your motivations – those things that you care most about and love to do.

3. **A**bilities

   These are the natural talents or abilities that you were born with. Some examples of these abilities include musical ability, athletic ability, mechanical ability, intellectual ability, artistic ability, writing ability, and communication ability.

4. **P**ersonality

It is quite obvious that God loves variety – just look around! He created each of us with a unique combination of personality traits. God made some introverts and some extroverts. He made some people who like routine and those who love variety. He made some people whose natural response is thinking and others who engage the world with their feelings.

5. **E**xperiences

Throughout the course of our lives, we have been shaped by a wide variety of experiences, both positive and negative. Many of these experiences were beyond our control. But God has allowed them for his purpose of moulding us. These experiences include:

  a. Family experiences: What are some of the things you learned as you grew up in your family?
  b. Educational experiences: What subjects in school did you enjoy the most?
  c. Vocational experiences: What are some of the jobs you had that you were especially effective in?
  d. Spiritual experiences: What are some of the most meaningful times you've had with God?
  e. Painful experiences: What problems/trials have you faced and learned from?

Rick Warren, the pastor who wrote *The Purpose Driven Life* and developed the SHAPE tool, says, "You will be most effective when you use your *spiritual gifts* and *abilities* in the area of your *heart's desire*, and in a way that best expresses your *personality* and *experiences*."[57]

From *The Discipler's Toolkit* | © Mark A. Olander | Published by Oasis International Ltd.

STOP AND REFLECT:

Using the explanations above, take some time to explore your own SHAPE.

My spiritual gifts:

_____

_____

_____

My heart:

_____

_____

_____

My abilities:

_____

_____

_____

My personality:

_____

_____

_____

My experiences:

_____

_____

_____

What are some ways you see these aspects of your SHAPE influencing how you engage as a Christian?

_____

_____

_____

_____

_____

_____

_____

_____

_____

_____

_____

_____

THE STORY OF AN ENGAGED DISCIPLE

Unlike Adelino, Peter Mualuko Kisulu shows us what it means to be engaged as a believer. God miraculously rescued Peter from demon-possession when he was a teenager. Later, he accepted Jesus Christ as his personal Saviour and began sharing his faith with relatives and friends. Growing in his relationship with Christ, he discovered that God had called him to be a missionary to unreached tribes that they too might hear the gospel message and become Christians.[58]

Peter initially served among his own people, the Kamba tribe in central Kenya. Later he was invited to join a medical missionary from overseas who was working in Turkana in northern Kenya. He knew that it would not be easy to live and work among the Turkana people whose tribal customs, diet, and lifestyle were very different from his own. Nevertheless, Peter sensed that God was calling him to be a missionary among them. When God reminded him of the Great Commission, he decided to go to Turkana. He later wrote:

> I had to accept the fact that the Turkana community was on the list of the people for whom Jesus Christ died on the cross, and that it would be the responsibility of the Holy Spirit, not mine, to change them. Mine would merely be to proclaim and to teach God's Word, helping them as much as I could in every possible way.[59]

Peter served as a missionary in Turkana for 17 years before retiring. During that time God used him to establish 15 churches, medical clinics, and schools in Turkana. Peter wrote, "The Lord has really done marvellous things using me, a weak and poor vessel, with little education. May glory be to him, he who enabled me to persevere through hardship and temptations."[60]

The writers of the *Africa Study Bible* challenge us to be willing to go with the gospel message wherever God might choose to send us. They write:

> *Ubuntu* [is] a word from Bantu languages in southern and eastern Africa that cannot be translated well into English. *Ubuntu* communicates the essence of being a human –"I am what I am because of who we all are." Jesus calls us to love people of all tribes and races. We must love them so much that we can even leave home and take the message of Jesus to nations that we used to look down upon (Matthew 19:29). One way we can show *ubuntu* is by asking our churches to send men and women as missionaries. That will not be easy. It will require much prayer and much giving. Perhaps the missionaries will suffer. But we Christians have true *ubuntu*, and we even love the people that others tell us to look down on.[61]

Today God is looking for obedient disciples who are available for him to use wherever he sends them. Are you among them?

PART II. THE THREE LEVELS OF MAKING DISCIPLES

Now that we've identified four phases of disciple making, we need to consider the setting or context in which this disciple-making process can take place. There are three basic tiers at which making disciples can take place. Each has its own method or ways of going about the task. One takes place in the context of a local church on a congregational level. A small group is the context for the second method. And the third takes place on an individual or one-on-one level.

Each method has merit, and they are not mutually exclusive. In fact, we have found that a combination of the three methods is the best overall approach.

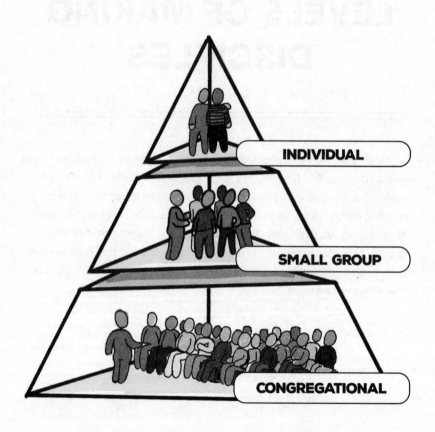

INDIVIDUAL

SMALL GROUP

CONGREGATIONAL

7

The Congregational Method of Disciple Making

In the context of a local church, there are many ways to engage in disciple making. Some are through preaching, but others are done by laypeople in the church. Certainly, the pastor needs to be leading by example, but others in the church must be involved as well. The following case study of a fictional church helps clarify how this might work.

A DISCIPLE-MAKING CHURCH STORY

Imagine the concerns of Pastor Barnabas, pastor of a local evangelical church in a West African country, who became increasingly concerned that many of the members of his church were "Dead Sea Christians". In other words, the pastor observed that his congregation was *taking in* a lot but *giving out* very little. They were faithful in attending Sunday morning services at the church but were not actively involved in church ministries or in reaching out to non-Christians in their community. His impression was that his church members were Sunday Christians but not Great Commission Christians. Pastor Barnabas was also concerned that the church members weren't reading or studying their Bibles during the week. He noted that they mostly just waited for Sunday mornings to be fed spiritually by the pastor's sermons. They were not fishing; they were simply waiting for someone to give them fish!

Pastor Barnabas met with the elders of the church and shared these concerns with them. The elders all agreed that these were definite needs in their church. The pastor suggested that the church become more intentional about making disciples. He challenged the leaders to help him take action.

One of the pastor's first steps was a *congregational method*; he preached a sermon series with the theme "True Discipleship". He used selected passages from the Gospels as the texts for his sermons.

What other types of sermon series might a pastor choose?

Preach a Series of Messages on Discipleship Topics

Christians need to be introduced to topics which deal with various aspects of the Christian life. A pastor can do a personal study on a variety of topics and then do a series of sermons on them. Some topics a pastor could preach on include:

- How to be sure you are a Christian

- The cost of discipleship

- The characteristics of a true disciple of Christ

- Don't waste your life – invest it!

- How to know God's will for your life

- How Jesus trained the 12 disciples

- Being a disciple maker

- How to give your life to things of eternal value

Preach a Series of Messages on the Balanced Christian Life

Another practical thing a local pastor can do is to prepare and preach a series of sermons that expose his congregation to topics about living a successful and balanced Christian life. The "Chair Illustration" (Resource G) provides an overall framework for this kind of message series. Potential sermon topics a pastor could address include:

- Making Christ the centre of your life

- How to get to know God's Word

- How to pray effectively

- How to share your faith

- Why we need one another

- The importance of being an obedient Christian

- Why fellowship with other Christians is important

- How to share your testimony

Preach a Series of Messages on Biblical Characters

Christians have much to learn from the stories of individual lives in the Bible. The apostle Paul makes reference to this when he tells the Corinthian Christians, "These things happened to them as examples and were written down as warnings for us, on whom the culmination of the ages has come" (1 Corinthians 10:11). There are countless biblical characters that could be studied. People from both the Old and New Testaments to study include:

Old Testament	New Testament
Abraham	Matthew
Joseph	Simon Peter
Moses	Thomas
Joshua	Judas
Caleb	Mary Magdalene
Achan	Paul
Naomi	Barnabas
Ruth	John Mark
David	Luke
Boaz	Timothy
Esther	Titus

HAVE CHURCH MEMBERS SHARE THEIR PERSONAL TESTIMONIES DURING CHURCH SERVICES

Pastor Barnabas then decided, in addition to sermon series, to have individual church members share their personal testimonies in Sunday morning church services. The pastor trained one of his elders how to meet individually with each of them to provide guidelines for them to follow when they gave their testimonies. He would have each person write out his or her testimony so that he could read through it and offer any suggestions as to how to make it clearly understood. These testimonies that were shared in church were greatly appreciated. They helped non-Christians in attendance hear the gospel and greatly encouraged fellow believers in their walk with Christ.

Let's consider some important things to know about testimonies for a congregation.

There are multiple benefits from having Christians give their testimonies in church. For example, it provides them a friendly environment in which they can practice telling their personal story of salvation. The inclusion of testimonies during a church service is also a good way of sharing the gospel with non-believers who are visiting. Furthermore, Christians themselves are always encouraged when they hear how God has worked in the lives of their Christian brothers and sisters. It is a practical way of building one another up in the faith.

One potential problem with inviting people to share testimonies is that some individuals think they are supposed to preach to the congregation instead of sharing their story. Another possible problem is that some people take too long to give their testimony. It is actually more difficult to give a short testimony than a long one!

Therefore, it is important to teach people *how* to give their testimony. You can also assist people to write their own testimonies. Have them read it to you so you can offer any suggestions.

S. How to Share Your Testimony

Let's look at some basic guidelines to help people share their stories concisely and effectively. They start with the letters TESTIMONY to make them easier to remember.[62]

Tell it in 3 parts.

- *Before* I met Christ . . .
  Share one or two good and bad qualities about what you were like before you became a Christian.

- *How* I met Christ . . .
  Explain clearly how you heard the gospel and what you did to become a Christian.

- *After* I met Christ . . .
  Tell about two or three changes you have seen in your life since you became a Christian.

Explain in understandable terms.

- Use words and expressions that a non-Christian can understand. Avoid using words like *went forward*, *sanctified*, or *justification*.

Share – don't preach!

- Use first person pronouns like *I*, *me*, and *my*. Avoid using *you* and *your* as if you were preaching a sermon.

Try to keep it short.

- Limit your testimony to three to five minutes if possible. This will help keep your listeners' attention.

Include some verses of Scripture.

- Share a verse or two that was instrumental in helping you come to Christ. Share a verse that has been meaningful to you since meeting the Lord.

From *The Discipler's Toolkit* | © Mark A. Olander | Published by Oasis International Ltd.

Make Christ central.

- Focus on what Jesus has done and continues to do in your life. Remember, this is a testimony, not a chance to boast!

Omit unnecessary information.

- Too much detailed information will clutter your testimony. Do not mention specific names of churches, organizations, or individuals. Critical statements can potentially alienate your listeners.

Never apologize for your story.

- God will use your testimony to reach someone. Don't feel that your testimony is not as dramatic as someone else's. Every Christian's story is unique and that is okay.

Yield the results to God.

- Not everyone who hears your story will be ready to accept Christ right away. Be assured that your testimony will be used by God to help this person understand how Christ can change a person's life.

STOP AND REFLECT:

Read through Paul's testimony before King Agrippa as recorded by Luke in Acts 26:2-23. See how many of the nine guidelines listed in Resource S you can identify in his testimony. Can you use it as a guideline for writing your own testimony?

_____

_____

_____

_____

_____

_____

_____

_____

_____

CREATE ADULT BIBLE CLASSES OR SMALL GROUPS

Pastor Barnabas shifted from congregational methods to *small group methods* when one of the elders in the church, who was a teacher by profession, suggested that adult Bible classes should be held during the children's Sunday school class time. They started with one adult class which studied a book of the Bible, then moved on to other topics. Over the period of several months, the number of adults who attended these Sunday morning adult Bible classes grew significantly. Even the pastor was surprised how much interest there was in these adult classes!

Several months later, one of the church members, Gachara, approached Pastor Barnabas with the suggestion of home Bible study groups being organized. He told the pastor that he believed this could help laypeople become more knowledgeable of the Bible and more firmly established in their faith. Pastor Barnabas said, "That's an *excellent* idea! Would *you* be willing to organize a small group ministry for our church?" Gachara agreed to do it if that the pastor would help him train group leaders. His first step was to recruit individuals who were willing to become small group leaders. This group of potential leaders met for several weeks to learn how to be effective group leaders.

Once the small group leader training was completed, members of the church were given the opportunity to join small groups led by the trained individuals. From the pulpit, the pastor strongly urged the church members to seriously consider joining one of the groups. Each of the small groups met once a week in the home of the leader or one of the other group members. The small group coordinator met together with the group leaders once every two months to give them an opportunity to share with one another how their groups were doing. They also shared ideas that could help one another respond to any difficulties or challenges they were encountering as leaders of their groups.

Let's consider some important things to know about Bible classes or study groups.

Have Adult Bible Classes on Sunday Morning

Adult classes could meet prior to the morning worship service, or while the children are in their Sunday school classes. We don't recommend don't using the term "Sunday school" for the adults because of the association with a children's activity. Adult Bible classes or Bible study groups are better names.

Adult classes could study a wide variety of interesting and relevant topics such as: 1) How to strengthen your marriage, 2) Being a godly parent, 3) How to raise teenagers, or 4) How to grow spiritually. They could also choose to study specific books of the Bible. There are 66 possibilities!

Regardless of the topic or book studied, teachers should strive to make these classes interactive by encouraging discussion, not just presenting content. Research shows that adults learn best when given the opportunity to engage in discussion. The process of communicating their thoughts and formulating questions solidifies ideas in the minds of adult learners. The worship service provides the opportunity to hear a sermon, but the class time should give the opportunity to dialogue with other adult learners.

As this is written, one vibrant, growing local church in the city of Nairobi, Kenya, has adult Bible classes that meet every Sunday morning during the children's Sunday school hour. This is one of the reasons the church is growing strong spiritually. There are currently two classes meeting, one class that focuses on discipleship topics and another class that usually studies either a book of the Bible or a helpful book by a Christian author. This class is very interactive because it is led by a teacher who is intentional about engaging all the class members in discussion.

Another actual church in Nairobi has a well-organized programme of Bible study classes which meet on Sunday mornings during the Sunday school time. This church has three adult classes attended by nearly 100 members! The class teachers are either pastors or laypeople from the church. Many of the adults in the church are eager to participate in these learning opportunities.

Encourage Members to Read the Bible Together

If you aren't able to organize teachers for classes, you can still encourage your congregation to read the Bible together. Pastor David Helm motivated his church members to read and study their Bibles during the week and not just at church on Sundays. He challenged each believer to regularly meet with one other person for a set length of time to read through and discuss God's Word. His book, *One to One Bible Reading,* contains several easy-to-photocopy sheets of questions to guide people in doing this.

You can also encourage your members to read the Bible with people in other churches or through other ministries. For example, several years ago a small group of Christian women in Nairobi began a Bible Study Fellowship for women from several different churches in the city. The women meet in one of the churches once a week. A team of Christian women leads the study to help other women learn how to study God's Word and apply it to their lives. Assignments are given each week, and the ladies come prepared for the next meeting. Each weekly meeting begins with a teaching time led by one of the leaders. Then the large group is divided into several small groups. Members discuss the biblical text and explore life applications. This method uses Bible Study Fellowship resources and invites women from many churches, reducing the burden for each church to create its own women's Bible study programme. The women also enjoy the fellowship of believers beyond their church.

ORGANIZE A DISCIPLESHIP PROGRAMME IN YOUR CHURCH

In Wadge and Carter's book entitled *Discipleship,* they describe a realistic way of organizing a discipleship programme in a local church. Here are the steps they recommend:

1. *Define clearly* our overall objectives. What is the overall purpose of having a discipleship programme?

2. *Understand* the way things are at the present time. What, if anything, is currently happening for discipleship training at your church?
3. *Write* down the things that need to be done. Be specific.
4. *List* equipment and materials that will be needed to have such a programme. This would primarily be Bible study books or other study helps.
5. *Appoint* a discipleship coordinator who will give overall guidance for the programme.
6. *Establish* a discipleship committee to work together in making decisions.
7. *Provide* training for those would wish to become disciple makers. Match young believers with older, more mature believers.
8. *Acquire* the needed discipleship materials (e.g., Bible study books). Don't hesitate to have people buy their own Bible study or discipleship books. People tend to value things more if they have to pay at least a portion of the cost of the materials.
9. *Engage* disciple makers with new believers.
10. *Evaluate regularly* the overall effectiveness of the programme, then make any necessary changes.[63]

These are very useful steps to establishing a discipleship programme. However, there is a potential danger if a local church believes that simply instituting a discipleship programme will fully address the need for disciple making. In his book *The Lost Art of Disciple Making*, LeRoy Eims makes this important observation:

> Why are fruitful, dedicated, mature disciples so rare? The biggest reason is that all too often we have relied on programs or materials or some other thing to do the job.
>
> The ministry is to be carried on by people, not programs. It is to be carried out by some*one* and not by some *thing*. Disciples cannot be mass produced. We cannot drop people into a "program" and see disciples emerge at the end of the production line. It takes time to make disciples.

It takes individual, personal attention. It takes hours of prayer for them. It takes patience and understanding to teach them how to get into the Word of God for themselves, how to feed and nourish their souls, and by the power of the Holy Spirit how to apply the Word to their lives. And it takes being an example to them of all of the above.[64]

STOP AND REFLECT:

In what ways does the case study of the disciple-making church illustrate the concept of the congregational method of disciple making?

_____

_____

_____

_____

_____

_____

_____

_____

_____

_____

_____

In Pastor Barnabas's story, we saw him moving from _congregational to small group to individual methods_ as he recruited one of the church elders to help him lead a training course for individuals in the church who had a desire to learn how to become disciple makers. This group met together for 90 minutes on Saturday mornings at the church. They studied the workbook entitled *Disciple Making in the African Church*. Each member was responsible to buy his or her own copy of the workbook. The group members were encouraged to look for individuals they could begin discipling even while they were going through their study of the workbook.

The story of Pastor Barnabas's local church congregation contains five basic components: 1) Sunday morning sermons on discipleship topics, 2) occasional personal testimonies in church services, 3) adult Bible classes on Sunday mornings, 4) growth groups led by trained small group leaders, and 5) a training course for those wanting to learn how to become disciple makers. These five components provided a variety of learning opportunities for church members to become involved depending upon their level of personal interest and commitment.

STOP AND REFLECT:

Does your local church currently have any kind of discipleship programme? If so, how can it be improved?

If your church does not currently have a discipleship programme, how would you design one that would be appropriate and realistic for your local church?

_____

_____

_____

_____

_____

_____

_____

_____

_____

_____

_____

8
The Small Group Method of Disciple Making

Some years ago, my wife and I (Mark) were living in a large city which had four sizeable universities. Over the years we were able to meet quite a number of the university students. Among the students we met, I found several that were interested in meeting together to study God's Word and encourage one another in our faith and walk with God. We began to meet together on a regular basis to fellowship, study, and pray.

These students came from four African countries: Kenya, Burkina Faso, Liberia, and Zambia. Sometimes we sang together in churches or local events. Twice we had weekend retreats together. It was a wonderful opportunity for all of us to help one another grow spiritually. To the best of my knowledge, each of these men is walking with the Lord today and investing his life in others as a disciple maker.

THE FOUR MAIN COMPONENTS OF A SMALL GROUP

A Kenyan writer named Nebert Mtange suggests that the small group method of discipleship seems especially appropriate in many African contexts:

Discipleship must find its home in groups, just as Jesus nurtured a group of twelve apostles for ministry. An African, who exercises love in a group by greetings, a visit, hospitality, and even prayer, needs to be encouraged and helped to anchor all the good actions in scripture.[65]

On the other hand, since Mtange points out that Jesus used the small group method, that also suggests that the small group method is our model in any culture! As disciple makers, we need to be trained to make disciples by leading small Bible study groups.

There are four elements or components that effective small groups have in common. Each aspect is important. A healthy, maturing small group will show evidence of spiritual nurture, corporate worship, mutual fellowship, and intentional mission.

Spiritual nurture is being instructed in the knowledge of God and his Word. Christians need to study the Word of God in order for spiritual growth to take place.

Corporate worship is when Christians glorify and praise God as a body of brothers and sisters in Christ. This usually takes the form of singing and praying together.

Mutual fellowship is encouraging and affirming one another as members of the body of Christ. We all need encouragement as we travel on our spiritual pilgrimage. And we also need others to affirm us and even correct us when needed.

Intentional mission is when Christians reach out to others outside the group. This requires being observant of the needs of others in the community and having a burden to help others spiritually and physically.

ATTRIBUTES OF A DISCIPLE MAKER

Joyce Landorf, in her book entitled *Balcony People*, suggests that we will discover two kinds of people in our life. Most of us fall somewhere on the spectrum between the evaluator and the affirmer types. Evaluators are those who tend to look only at performance. They are critical of the faults and mistakes of others and endeavour to influence others by judging and correcting them. Affirmers, on the other hand, show unconditional acceptance and affirmation. They focus more on what people can become than on what they were in the past or what they are like at the present time. They discover qualities and see the potential in individuals.[66] As disciple makers, our role is that of affirmers. We must, as Scripture says, always speak the truth in love.

> **As disciple makers, our role is that of affirmers. We must, as Scripture says, always speak the truth in love.**

Our role as a group leader is key to the success of our Bible study group. Ron Davis's excellent book, *Mentoring: The Strategy of the Master*, includes a helpful discussion regarding the attributes of a mentor. These qualities certainly apply to disciple makers who want to be affirmers. Here is a summary of the seven attributes he identifies:

1. Be honest and direct when confronting. Be sure to address the issue at hand.
2. When you confront, demonstrate love and acceptance.
3. Be specific, avoid speaking in generalizations when confronting.
4. Demonstrate empathy as you confront.
5. Build on the learner's strengths, gifts, and character through positive encouragement.
6. Affirm in public, correct in private.
7. Build an allegiance to relationships, not to issues. [67]

While we find his ideas helpful, it is important to remember that the application of these principles may differ from culture to culture. In Côte d'Ivoire for example, there is a cultural structure for confronting to which a wise disciple maker will adapt. A face-to-face, direct conversation about any important subject is insulting. The message will probably not be received, and the relationship might be destroyed. As disciple makers, it is our responsibility to learn how to have tender-tough conversations, how to speak truth in love, in the context where we are making disciples.

STOP AND REFLECT:

Describe a time someone affirmed you. What are some good ways to speak the truth in love in your culture?

_____

_____

_____

_____

_____

_____

_____

_____

_____

_____

Other attributes of a disciple maker are courage and integrity. As John Maxwell once said, "People may teach what they know, but they reproduce what they are."[68] Don't be afraid to fail. Remember that failure can be as important as success if we learn from our mistakes! We have to "walk our talk" – making sure that we practice what we teach. A good definition of integrity is doing the right thing even when no one is watching!

Our prayer life is crucial. Davis describes three potential barriers to prayer: *ritualism*, which can take the form of standardized and memorized prayers or certain positions and times of the day which when done in a rote fashion can be devoid of meaning; *repetition*, which can be a vain effort when individuals repeat set prayers without giving thought to what they are saying to God; and *pride*, which can motivate a person to pray in a way they hope will impress others.

Failure can be as important as success if we learn from our mistakes!

An effective disciple maker also needs discernment and wisdom when helping a disciple make decisions. James 1:5 instructs us to ask God for wisdom and he promises to provide the wisdom we need. When advising a disciple on what to do when faced with tough decisions in "grey areas", Davis advises referring to these five questions: (1) Will engaging in this activity help me to emulate Christ and walk as he would walk? (2) Will this activity hinder or help me in my goal of becoming more like Christ? (3) If I am involved in this activity, is my witness to the world going to be enhanced or diminished? (4) Will this activity build me up spiritually or will it bring me down? and (5) Would my involvement in this activity be a good example for other Christian friends?

Part of our motivation as disciple makers should be a desire to energize others for service, Davis says. Our agenda is to help facilitate the growth and development of the new believer. Recognize the blessing of constructive criticism. As one proverb says, we need to have the mind of a scholar, the heart of a child, and the hide of a rhinoceros. Misunderstandings and criticisms are inevitable, but we should not allow them to derail us from our mentoring pursuit.[69]

BASIC PRINCIPLES OF DISCIPLE MAKING IN A GROUP CONTEXT

As you can see in the story at the beginning of this chapter, disciple making can take place when a person disciples a group of people instead of just one individual at a time. When making disciples in a group context, there are some basic principles which we should consider. We begin by actively looking for individuals in whom we can invest our lives.[70] It is important to prayerfully select those who join our group. Jesus spent an entire night in prayer before selecting his apostles. It is a good idea to start with a relatively small group. Jesus, for example, worked with a group of 12 people. When we disciple a small group of individuals, we are using our time expediently.

We should require mutual commitment. It is good to set the bar high for expectations. People generally respond well to challenges. Your expectations must be clear from the start. Disciples need to know what they can expect of us as their group leader and what we expect of them.

It is helpful to begin with the end in mind. In other words, agree upon a tentative length of time you will be meeting together. The time frame includes how long each meeting will be and how many weeks or months the meetings will continue. It is important that we give our time and energy sacrificially to help those we are discipling, being sensitive to their needs instead of simply following our own agenda. Having an overall plan for disciple making is good, but we also need to be flexible.

God's Word must be central as we disciple individuals in our group. Biblical principles should be shared with them instead of simply our own opinions or ideas. (In Resource Y, we'll give you some examples of biblical passages you might use when dealing with various issues or needs that disciples might have.)

It is extremely important to pray regularly for each of the individuals in our group on our own. Furthermore, we should spend time praying with them about their needs. We teach them how to pray by our example. Remember how Jesus taught his disciples to pray (Luke 11:1-4). We often learn best through watching others do something. Always endeavour to set a good example for new believers to follow.

Another important principle is to teach along the way of life, always watching for teachable moments in disciples' lives. For example, consider the time when Jesus taught his disciples about servant-leadership at the Last Supper (John 13:1-17). Their worldly understanding of leadership needed to be corrected by seeing what godly leadership looked like.

Finally, we should anticipate spiritual multiplication in the lives of disciples. It is an appropriate expectation for us to have that they will, in turn, disciple others.[71]

T. Communication Skills for Group Leaders

Discipleship group leaders need training to lead small groups. Here are important communication skills small group leaders should develop, adapted from Judy Hamlin's book, *The Small Group Leaders Training Course*: [72]

1. *Listening* – focusing on the person who is talking; carefully hearing what is being said.
2. *Attending* – demonstrating that you are carefully paying attention by facing the person, talking and saying things like "yes", "really", or "how interesting".
3. *Seeking information and opinions* – calling on people by name, using questions to draw out quiet group members: "Mueni, have you had an experience with evangelism you would feel comfortable sharing with us?"
4. *Clarifying* – asking clarifying questions such as "I'm not sure I understand what you mean. Could you rephrase that for me please?"
5. *Paraphrasing* – restating what another has said, "This is what I thought heard you say. Am I on the right track?"
6. *Justifying* – asking people to give reasons for what they have said, "Help us see how you drew that from the passage we are studying."
7. *Re-directing* – encouraging group members to talk to one another; "Mutuku, how would you respond to Mueni's question?"

8. *Extending* – adding to or expanding a line of thought; "Does anyone have anything to add to what has been said?"
9. *Summarizing* – briefly highlighting and summarizing what has been said so far; outlining where the discussion has been and where it should be going: "So far we have talked about what Jesus meant by Jerusalem and Judea. Shall we look at what he meant by mentioning Samaria and the ends of the earth?"
10. *Affirming* – recognizing a group member's contributions with statements like, "Thank you for that helpful insight." or "That's a very interesting observation! Thanks for pointing that out."
11. *Being personal* – using the personal pronoun "I", for example, "I feel" or "I think", not "some people think or believe", being specific when expressing your thoughts.
12. *Being teachable* – showing that you want to learn from others' insights and ideas, for instance: "That's interesting. I've never thought of it from that perspective before. Tell us more."

From *The Discipler's Toolkit* | © Mark A. Olander | Published by Oasis International Ltd.

DEALING WITH POTENTIAL PROBLEMS IN A SMALL GROUP

It's not unusual to encounter problems within a small group. Here are some of the most common ones and some suggestions for how to deal with them.

When *talkative members* dominate the discussions, try sitting next to them rather than directly across from them. This avoids direct eye contact with them, and they will be less likely to respond to every question. You can also say, "That's great! Now let's hear from someone who hasn't had a chance to comment yet." We've found that the most effective way of dealing with a talkative person is to speak to him or her privately and ask them to help you involve others in the discussions. Encourage them to intentionally hold back a little to give others an opportunity to participate.

You may have *silent members* who rarely, if ever, say anything. Questions directed to those who haven't yet talked may draw them out, but be careful to ask them questions you are sure they can answer. That will help them gain confidence so they continue to contribute more to the group discussions.

Unprepared members can be challenged to come prepared next time, but be careful not to embarrass them or they may stop coming. Encourage them that they will benefit much more if they come prepared.

If you have *argumentative members*, try to find something good in what they are saying. Then, build on their good insights as you respond in a loving way to their aggressive comments. Seek to be patient and gracious without being defensive or argumentative.

When *incorrect answers* or heretical comments are put forth in the discussions, it is important that you set the record straight. You can do this by asking, "How does this passage support that idea?" Or you can ask for other group members' comments. If you don't correct wrong information, group members may believe the comments are accurate.

Difficult questions will sometimes be raised. In that case, ask other group members what they think. Someone else in the group might have an answer to the questions. If you as the leader don't know the answer, admit it! Determine to find a response and bring it to the group in the future.

Controversial subjects may be raised. It is usually best to graciously defer the discussion about those topics to another time. Be careful to not be dogmatic. Acknowledge their interest in these subjects but don't let these topics sidetrack your discussions.

Absent members can create a problem. It is a good idea for you or someone else in the group to contact them and communicate that the group has missed them.

Non-responsive groups happen. It can be very discouraging for a group leader to encounter a lethargic group. Show enthusiasm and pray for renewed motivation in the hearts of the group members. You can also try to help them see the importance of what is being studied and its application to their lives.[73]

STOP AND REFLECT:

Have you ever been a part of a small group where you observed some problems due to either poor leadership or attitudes and actions of some group members? If so, how were these problems dealt with?

_____

_____

_____

_____

_____

_____

_____

_____

_____

_____

_____

THE PARABLE OF THE DYSFUNCTIONAL BIBLE STUDY GROUP

There once was a church member, Ahmed, who asked his pastor if he could start a Bible study group that would meet in his home. The pastor responded enthusiastically, "By all means! That would be great!" The following Sunday morning the pastor announced the new Bible study group to the congregation and told them to let him know if they were interested in joining. Ahmed and the pastor were delighted when 13 people signed up indicating their desire to participate.

When they met the first time, the Ahmed suggested that they go around the circle and introduce themselves. Unfortunately, one of the members of the group took so long telling about himself that they ran out of time and had to finish the meeting before everyone had a chance to introduce themselves. Ahmed could already see there might be a problem with this talkative member because his eagerness to talk dominated the group.

The following week when the group met, he made sure that everyone had a chance to introduce themselves by limiting the amount of time each person could talk. Then, Ahmed told the group that next week they would begin a study of the book of James.

During the next session, Ahmed did *all* the talking because he was determined to pass onto the group members all that he had learned as he had prepared for this first study in James. In reality, he simply taught a Bible lesson instead of leading a Bible study. The entire time was taken up with Ahmed's teaching. He didn't allow any time for the group members to ask questions or make comments. The group members listened passively to the lesson Ahmed taught. There was no group discussion. The group had no energy and was essentially lifeless. For all practical purposes, the group members had listened to a sermon. This was the pattern of each of the Bible study sessions.

Eventually, Ahmed observed that the group members were declining in enthusiasm for the group meetings. He decided to start using discussion questions in an effort to get the members more involved in discovering biblical truth. Unfortunately, the questions he asked were mostly ones that could be answered with either "yes" or "no". The answers to a few of the questions were so obvious that no one bothered to respond. Despite this, there were some responses to Ahmed's questions, but "Mr. Talkative" was always first, responding before anyone else could say anything. The other members of the group eventually gave up trying to share their comments because "Mr. Talkative" monopolized the discussion time.

Attendance at the Bible study began to gradually decline. Ahmed knew it was probably because of the one group member who talked too much.

STOP AND REFLECT:

What does this example teach us about what a leader should avoid doing?

_____

_____

_____

_____

_____

_____

_____

_____

_____

He decided to meet individually with the person. First, Ahmed commended "Mr. Talkative" for his enthusiasm and eagerness to participate in the group discussions. He said, "I wish _all_ the other group members were as enthusiastic as _you_ are!" After affirming the group member, Ahmed asked if he would help him get other members to participate more in the discussions during their meetings. He encouraged him to intentionally hold back, giving other members a chance to participate and share their insights. "Mr. Talkative" said he would do his best to restrain himself from trying to answer every question. This greatly helped more people to get involved in the discussions. The result was growing enthusiasm and life in the group meetings.

Then Ahmed began to do a better job of writing good discussion questions to use while facilitating the Bible study. Before the meetings, he took time to write down a variety of observation, interpretation, and application questions that he could use to guide the discussions of the biblical passages they were studying. These carefully designed questions helped the discussions be more profitable and enjoyable for all the members. It provided useful structure for the Bible study discussion time. As a result, the Bible study group was transformed from being a largely dysfunctional group into a very functional and beneficial one.

STOP AND REFLECT:

Ahmed gradually made some changes that eventually improved the effectiveness of the Bible study group. What were the changes that he made?

_____

_____

_____

_____

_____

_____

_____

_____

As seen in the preceding parable, good discussion questions which engage group members are essential if a Bible study group is to be effective. So how do we go about developing good discussion questions?

U. Asking Questions

Here are some excellent guidelines for the development and use of discussion questions, from Judy Hamlin's training manual. She used the acrostic ASKING QUESTIONS:[74]

Avoid questions that result in "yes" or "no" answers.
These questions don't generate any meaningful discussions. It is better to ask questions that require more reflective and thoughtful responses.

Start with easy, nonthreatening questions.
These will help the group members to enter into discussion sooner. If you begin the study with questions that are difficult to answer, group members may be reluctant to respond. It is better to begin with questions that are relatively easy to answer like observation questions.

Keep the discussion moving.
Don't let it get bogged down on topics. It is your responsibility as group leader to keep the discussion moving along, not dragging.

Invite sharing of information and opinions.
Allow plenty of time for group members to contribute to the discussion. Don't be afraid of silence. Give people time to think about the questions. Resist the temptation to answer your own questions when group members don't respond right away.

Never make fun of a response.
If a group member makes a comment or gives an answer and the leader or anyone else makes fun of her or him, the person may stop participating in discussions or stop attending the meetings altogether. People need affirmation, not mocking.

Even if a group member gives an incorrect answer, be careful to correct him or her graciously.

Give enough time for people to respond.
Be willing to tolerate times of silence while people are thinking how to respond. Avoid the temptation to answer your own questions. If necessary, you may need to rephrase a question when you sense that people have not fully understood it.

Questions should focus on the biblical text.
That is to say we should focus primarily on what the Bible says and means. We need to get below the surface information and dig deeper into Scripture. Challenge group members to think!

Use a variety of questions.
Include observation questions (What does the Bible say?), interpretation questions (What does it mean?), and application questions (How does it apply to our lives today?). For example, an observation question is "What did Jesus do for his disciples just before he died?" An interpretation question would be, "Why do you think Peter resisted when Jesus wanted to wash his feet?" An application question could be, "What is one action you could take to serve someone in your family this week?" Generally speaking, it is good to begin with observation questions, then move into interpretation, and end with application questions.

Explore possible applications.
Have the group suggest general applications to everyday life. Don't simply tell them how the biblical truths apply, but challenge them to think for themselves.

Steer the discussion.
Don't let the discussion get off track by chasing "rabbit trails". It is your responsibility as the group leader to keep the discussion focused.

Try to avoid double negative questions.
This type of question is really confusing to group members and they won't know how to answer them. An example of a double negative question is "Why didn't Peter misunderstand who Jesus was?" Instead, ask, "Why did Peter understand who Jesus was?"

Inspire and encourage group members.
Be positive about their contributions to the discussion. Motivate them with your enthusiasm; it's contagious!

One thought at a time.
Keep the discussion focused on one question at a time. Don't let it become too complicated. Avoid confusing group members by discussing multiple topics at the same time.

Name people, if it would be helpful.
There are times when it may be helpful to call upon people by name when looking for an answer to a question. However, it is advisable to not do this very often because group members may begin waiting for someone to be called upon to answer or comment. Encourage them to answer of their own initiative.

Summarize the conclusions.
Before you move from one topic to another, summarize what has been discussed. A summary statement from you as leader is also important at the end of your discussion time to bring closure to the Bible study.

From *The Discipler's Toolkit* | © Mark A. Olander | Published by Oasis International Ltd.

GENERAL GUIDELINES FOR STRUCTURING SMALL GROUPS

As much as possible, restrict the size of groups to no more than 12 people. In a larger group, discussion becomes more difficult. Encourage groups to meet on a regular basis. Meeting weekly is preferable, but not always possible. Plan to meet at least every two weeks if possible.

Share prayer needs and allow sufficient time to bring these needs before the Lord without letting it take all the time. Praying for one another is a wonderful way to hold up and support each other.

Discuss biblical topics or passages using printed Bible study materials or other materials you have developed yourself. Don't hesitate to ask members to pay for their own Bible study materials if they need to be purchased. People tend to value things more when they have to pay for them.

Ultimately, the goal is for Christians to become "self-feeders" so they don't have to rely solely upon others to "feed" them God's Word when they attend church gatherings. Disciples need to learn how to fish and not simply be given fish.[75]

Steve Smith's and Ying Kai's book entitled *T4T: A Discipleship Re-Revolution* shares an encouraging testimony about the church planting movement in various places in the world. They show that one key factor in a successful church planting movement is helping Christians learn how to study the Word of God and apply it to their lives, and mention how the inductive type of Bible study is one effective way to do this.

In these methods, as the Holy Spirit guides your group members in their study of God's Word, they will gain understanding of the Bible and identify practical applications to life based upon what they have discovered from the biblical passage.[76] Jesus promised to send his disciples the Spirit of truth to guide them into all truth. The Spirit does that by speaking only what he receives from God the Father (John 16:13). Jesus further said the Spirit would teach his disciples all things and help them remember Jesus's teaching (John 14:26). The Holy Spirit has an important role in helping us learn from biblical texts. Let's look at two methods that help disciples learn to fish for themselves:

V. Discovery Bible Study Method for Groups

A very effective method of group Bible study is the Discovery Bible Study.[77] This method can be used with either literate or non-literate people and follows the following pattern:

1. The group leader either reads or tells a Bible story to the other group members. If the group members are literate and have their own Bibles, they can either follow in their Bibles while the leader reads or take turns reading themselves as they go through the story.
2. The leader then invites members of the group to share with others what they learned from the story. The group members take turns telling the story in their own words while the others listen to make sure the story is told accurately.
3. The leader asks the members to think of someone they can tell the story to sometime before the next group meeting.
4. At the following meeting, each member is asked to report to the others about how it went when he or she told the story to another individual.
5. After that sharing time, the group leader introduces a new story from the Bible and the cycle repeats itself.

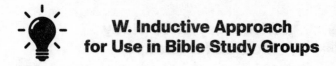

W. Inductive Approach for Use in Bible Study Groups

Another very effective method of group Bible study is the inductive method. We're using the term *inductive* here to mean that the group members come up with answers together as they ask relevant questions of the biblical text.

It is the leader's responsibility to guide the group members as they ask and answer various questions of the text. Here is one example of a useful set of questions:

1. What is the passage saying?
2. Is there anything you don't understand about the passage?
3. What does this passage teach us about God?
4. What does this passage tell us that we should do?
5. Who can we share this with this week?[78]

Questions like these can be used with virtually any passage in the Bible. It is advisable to study various biblical passages that will enable the group members to gain a basic understanding of the Bible, God, Christ, salvation, and discipleship. It can be helpful to select a book of the Bible (for example, the Gospel of Mark) to study through as a group. This has the advantage of providing continuity and direction as the group studies God's Word.

POTENTIAL PROBLEMS AND TENSIONS IN MENTORING RELATIONSHIPS

Of course, problems and tensions may occur in disciple-making relationships, whether in a group context or in the one-on-one settings we will look at in the next chapter. Let's look at some of the most common potential problems and consider practical ways that you, as the leader, can either avoid them or deal with them if they arise.

A *betrayal of confidence* is extremely harmful. Make it a policy to always keep information confidential. *Incompatible personalities* make relationships difficult, so avoid this problem by not selecting people whose personalities clash with yours. The relationships will be unproductive if you have *inappropriate motives*; be committed, therefore, to making disciples of Jesus rather than disciples of yourself. Make sure there is no *hypocrisy* in your life, but rather that your life backs up what you are teaching. Disciple makers must lead by example.

> **Be committed to making disciples of Jesus rather than disciples of yourself.**

Disciples may have *pride* in their life which will prevent them from learning from you and others. If you perceive this problem, challenge the individual to develop a humble attitude which will enable them to learn and continue to grow toward spiritual maturity. An *unteachable* disciple will always make the process a struggle. Don't frustrate yourself and waste your time trying to disciple people with know-it-all attitudes.

Finally, disciples may demonstrate a *lack of cooperation*. In this case, stress the importance of following the leader's guidance. If a disciple doesn't cooperate, the process will be largely ineffective and both disciple maker and disciple will be wasting their time.

HELPING GROUP MEMBERS DEVELOP THEIR FULLEST POTENTIAL

One of our primary goals in disciple making is to help the individuals in our Bible study groups develop their potential. In David A. Stoddard's book, *The Heart of Mentoring*, he suggests several helpful principles.

Living is about giving of yourself to others, so open your world to the people you are discipling. It's your job to model character that show them what Christlikeness looks like. Affirm the values of spiritual growth and maturity. Help your group members align passion and work, turning personal values into practice. Comfort them by sharing the load.[79]

Stoddard says that making disciples is a process that requires perseverance. But making disciples plus reproduction equals legacy. Take, for instance, the legacy of Adeline Adeotan Sikuade Agbebi. She recognized the power of organizing groups of Christ-followers. She and her husband served with the Nigerian Baptist Convention. Adeline travelled far and wide to organize and encourage women's societies. She also had a passion for teaching children Bible verses and songs, whether in her house or under a tree. Old or young, she discipled believers to faithfully obey the Lord. Today she is remembered as the founding mother of the Women's Missionary Union.[80]

We, too, can make an impact when we begin the faithful work of small group discipleship. Start small today, and see what God will do!

STOP AND REFLECT:

Would you be willing to become a small group leader? Why or why not?

If you are currently leading or attending some form of a small Bible study group, how is it going? What is one piece of advice from this chapter that could improve your group?

_____

_____

_____

_____

_____

_____

_____

_____

_____

_____

_____

_____

_____

_____

_____

_____

_____

_____

_____

_____

_____

_____

9

The Individual Method of Disciple Making

In addition to the congregational and small group methods of disciple making, there is a third very effective method sometimes referred to as the individual method. This is also called the one-on-one method of disciple making, when an older, more mature Christian intentionally invests his or her life in the life of younger believer with the purpose of helping the young Christian grow as a disciple of Jesus.

A good example of this method of disciple making took place at an urban church in Nairobi. Abdoulaye, who was a recent convert from Islam, began attending this local church at the recommendation of a Christian friend. He had only been a Christian for several months when he first began attending. As a result of his defection from Islam to Christianity, Abdoulaye was kicked out of his home and denied a job in the family's businesses. Since he had no place to stay, he was initially allowed to lodge on the church grounds while looking for a place to live.

Meanwhile, one of the men in the church, John, took a special interest in this new Christian and began meeting with him to discuss the Bible and Christianity. They spent many hours together in Bible study and prayer. John helped Abdoulaye find a place to live and continued to regularly visit him to read God's Word, pray together, and encourage one another.

Sometime later, Abdoulaye was given an opportunity to take a discipleship training course offered by a Christian organization in the Nairobi area. He later earned a certificate in theology during a one-year course at a Bible school in a neighbouring country. During this year, John kept in touch with him, calling and exchanging messages. When Abdoulaye had an opportunity to return to Kenya, he always visited John.

He returned to Kenya when he had completed his studies and began serving in the church. Abdoulaye then joined a Christian para-church organization where part of his ministry involved visiting schools and sharing his own testimony of how God had saved him from the darkness of Islam and given him a new life in Christ. Meanwhile, John continued meeting with him regularly and communicating through phone calls. Their times together usually consisted of praying for one another, discussing Bible passages, and helping each other find ways to apply biblical truths to their lives.

Even today, these two men continue to meet occasionally to study God's Word and pray for one another. In a very strategic way, John has been a disciple maker in the life of the young convert to Christianity. The result of the disciple maker's involvement has been a vibrant and growing disciple of Christ. And the disciple maker himself has grown spiritually in the process of pouring his life into the life of the young Christian.

> **It is always a two-way street when we pour our lives into the lives of others.**

There are several important things we can learn from the example of this older Christian who discipled a new believer. Notice that John took the initiative to ask Abdoulaye if he wanted to meet together. Also note that he helped the young Christian with his physical needs (e.g., helping him find a place to live), not only his spiritual needs. Furthermore, we can see the importance of spending regular times together studying God's Word, applying God's Word, and praying for one another. Finally, notice that both of them grew spiritually. It is always a two-way street when we pour our lives into the lives of others.

The positive impact that an older, mature Christian can have upon the life of a younger Christian is illustrated in the following comment by Floyd McClung:

> When I think about those who have influenced me most in life, it's a few people who made a significant investment in me. These are men and women who believed in me and took time to impart to me what God had deposited in their lives. The goal of discipleship is not disseminating information, but life-on-life formation. I have heard a lot of great sermons in my days. I have read many excellent books. And I have interacted with world-class leaders. But what really changed my life were those who took the time to get to know me and mentor me.[81]

Indeed, from a distance you may be able to impress others, but it is only up close that are you able to impact their lives.

BIBLICAL EXAMPLES OF DISCIPLE-MAKING RELATIONSHIPS

Throughout the Bible, we find examples of people who discipled others. In the Old Testament, Moses discipled the leader who would follow him, Joshua (Exodus-Deuteronomy). Naomi discipled her daughter-in-law, Ruth (Ruth). Elijah discipled his protégé, Elisha (2 Kings). Eli discipled a child in his care, Samuel (1 Samuel). Nathan discipled King David (2 Samuel).

Continuing on in the New Testament, John the Baptist had a group of disciples (Luke 7:18; John 1:35). Jesus had 12 disciples (Mark 3:14-16), including Simon Peter. Apollos was a disciple of Priscilla and Aquila (Acts 18:24-26). Barnabas initially discipled Paul (Acts 9:26-30; 11:25-30) and later John Mark (Acts 15:36-41).

These discipleship relationships focused on various topics. These included encouragement (Moses and Joshua, Deuteronomy 31:7-8), discernment (Eli and Samuel, 1 Samuel 3:8), accountability (Nathan and David, 2 Samuel 12:1-23), wisdom in decision making

(Naomi and Ruth, book of Ruth), empowerment (Elijah and Elisha, 2 Kings 2:1-15), and correction (Priscilla and Aquila with Apollos, Acts 18:24-26).

HOW PAUL INVESTED HIS LIFE IN TIMOTHY

One of the clearest examples of a disciple maker in the Bible is the apostle Paul. Paul was a missionary and church planter, but he also spent time discipling individuals such as Silas, Titus, Epaphroditus, and Timothy. We have already seen how Paul took Timothy under his wing, building on the strong faith already planted in him by his mother Eunice and his grandmother Lois (2 Timothy 1:5). Paul invited Timothy to join him and Barnabas when they passed through Lystra on Paul's second missionary journey. A study of their relationship demonstrates several things Paul did in the process of discipling Timothy.

He *wrote* to him (1 & 2 Timothy); he *prayed* for him (2 Timothy 1:3); he *loved* him (2 Timothy 1:4); he *encouraged* him (2 Timothy 1:5-7); he *instructed* him (2 Timothy 1:13); he *showed* him how a disciple lives (2 Timothy 3:10-11); he *exhorted* him to disciple others (2 Timothy 2:2); he *took* him along in ministry (Acts 16:1-5); and he *sent* him to disciple other Christians (Philippians 2:19-24).

Paul, Eunice, and Lois demonstrated what Lois Semenye sees as the goals of Christian education: "Christian education passes the Christian faith from one generation to the next. It helps believers to make their faith their own and to live it out. Aided by the Holy Spirit who indwells every believer, it gives direction for every stage of life."[82]

BASIC ASPECTS OF DISCIPLESHIP

Keith Anderson and Randy Reese have written a very helpful book entitled *Spiritual Mentoring*. In their book, they identify five key aspects of spiritual mentoring or discipleship. The first aspect, *attraction*, is the art of beginning well. This is the initial phase of establishing the relationship. Attraction takes place when a person notices certain desirable qualities, skills, or attributes of someone else. This draws one person to another person who could be a potential mentor.[83]

A second aspect is *relationship*, developing trust and intimacy. In order for effective discipling to take place, it is crucial that the environment be safe and welcoming. To a certain extent, the discipleship relationship is one of friendship in which there is an element of trust.

Responsiveness is a third aspect, what we might call the spirit of teachability. A disciple needs to have a teachable spirit and an eagerness to learn. It is important for the disciple maker to know how to use good questions.

Accountability is another important aspect of disciple making. We all need someone to hold us accountable at every stage of our pilgrimage as Christians if we have a sincere desire to grow spiritually. We need someone to ask us the hard questions.

The final aspect that Anderson and Reese point out is the goal of spiritual mentoring or disciple making – *empowerment*. The disciple maker ultimately desires for a disciple to understand who God is, who the disciple is, and what God created the disciple to do with his or her life. The disciple maker desires to see the disciple exercise his or her God-given abilities and spiritual gifts in serving.

STOP AND REFLECT:

In which of these five aspects of spiritual mentoring do you need improvement?

_____

_____

_____

_____

_____

_____

_____

_____

X. Five Ps for Meeting with Individuals

What exactly do you do when you get together with someone in a discipling relationship? One simple way to know what to do is to remember five words that begin with the letter **P**.

1. **P**rogress
   Share progress since your last meeting together. How is she or he doing in general? Follow up on any assignment(s) so that you will be taken seriously when you give future assignments. Lead by example by making sure you also do the assignment.

1. **P**assage
   Study a passage of Scripture together. If you select a book of the Bible to study, discuss one portion of the book each time you meet. If you use Bible study material, it is best to both have a copy of the book to complete before you discuss it together.

2. **P**roblems
   Discuss any challenges each of you might be facing currently. This is not a counselling session, so you don't have to solve problems, but you will ask God to solve them.

3. **P**rayer
   Pray for each other regarding the requests you have just shared. It is always encouraging to hear someone else pray about your needs and concerns.

4. **P**lans
   Before you leave, agree on a time and place for your next meeting. Agree on what each of you should do to prepare you for your next meeting, such as answering the questions in the next chapter in the Bible study book you are using. You can always make adjustments if needed.

From *The Discipler's Toolkit* | © Mark A. Olander | Published by Oasis International Ltd.

GUIDELINES FOR THE DISCIPLE MAKER

In addition to knowing what to do in our regular meetings, there are guidelines to keep in mind as we engage in one-on-one disciple making. It is important to *pray often for the individual*. Pray about the specific needs he or she has shared with you. *Do some things together just to relax and have fun*. Times of Bible study together are obviously very important, but it is also important to do an activity together that you both enjoy.

Be observant and respond accordingly to the person's needs. For example, when you meet and sense that he or she is discouraged, look for ways to encourage the person. We may notice areas of their Christian lives that need attention. It is important for us to have a biblical basis for anything we say to them. It is not enough for us to simply offer our opinions or share our personal advice. In Resource Y, we have listed 20 topics that are examples of some of the needs growing Christians might have and some appropriate Scriptures to use. Then, *share your personal experiences*, both your successes and your failures. It is important to *have a plan but be flexible*. Be sensitive to God's curriculum for this person. Your plan should include opportunities to *serve together in ministry*. Take them along with you when you are engaging in ministry opportunities.

Finally, *set a good example* for them to follow. People often learn far more from our example than from what we tell them. In his book series on discipleship entitled *MasterLife*, Avery Willis emphasizes the importance of setting a good example for those we are discipling. He writes, "You cannot teach what you are not practicing any more than you can return from a place you've never been. Disciples learn to do what they see you do."

Several African proverbs and sayings clearly illustrate how we learn from the example of others. An Ashanti proverb says, "When you follow the path of your father, you learn to walk like him." A Ugandan proverb says, "If the owner of the land leads you, you cannot get lost." And Kenyans say, "If a leader limps, all the others start limping too."[84]

The apostle Paul reinforced the importance of setting a good example for others when he wrote to Timothy, "Don't let anyone look down upon you because you are young, but set an example for the believers in speech, in conduct, in love, in faith and in purity" (1 Timothy 4:12).

STOP AND REFLECT:

Why is it essential that a disciple maker set a good example for the one being discipled in terms of speech, actions, attitudes, beliefs, and thoughts?

_____

_____

_____

_____

_____

_____

_____

_____

_____

_____

_____

_____

_____

_____

_____

_____

_____

_____

_____

Y. Scriptures for Specific Problems

As you look at the passages we have listed below as examples, you may also think of additional Scripture verses that could be beneficial for individuals who need help in these areas of their lives. The important thing is that biblical principles be applied to life.

1. Having the right priorities
   "But seek first his kingdom and his righteousness, and all these things will be given to you as well" (Matthew 6:33).
2. Finding purpose in life
   "'For I know the plans I have for you,' declares the Lord, 'plans to prosper you and not to harm you, plans to give you hope and a future'" (Jeremiah 29:11).
3. Bearing spiritual fruit
   "But the fruit of the Spirit is love, joy, peace, forbearance, kindness, goodness, faithfulness, gentleness and self-control. Against such things there is no law" (Galatians 5:22-23).
4. Overcoming fear
   "So do not fear, for I am with you; do not be dismayed, for I am your God. I will strengthen you and help you; I will uphold you with my righteous right hand" (Isaiah 41:10).
5. Developing humility and gentleness
   "In the same way, you who are younger, submit yourselves to your elders. All of you, clothe yourselves with humility towards one another, because, 'God opposes the proud but shows favour to the humble.' Humble yourselves, therefore, under God's mighty hand that he may lift you up in due time" (1 Peter 5:5-6).
6. Making good decisions
   "If any of you lacks wisdom, you should ask God, who gives generously to all without finding fault, and it will be given to you" (James 1:5).

7. Developing a stronger prayer life
   "Do not be anxious about anything, but in every situation, by prayer and petition, with thanksgiving, present your requests to God. And the peace of God, which transcends all understanding, will guard your hearts and your minds in Christ Jesus" (Philippians 4:6-7).

8. Learning to have an attitude of gratitude
   "Rejoice always, pray continually, give thanks in all circumstances; for this is God's will for you in Christ Jesus" (1 Thessalonians 5:16-18).

9. Being aware of spiritual warfare
   "Finally, be strong in the Lord and in his mighty power. Put on the full armour of God, so that you can take your stand against the devil's schemes. For our struggle is not against flesh and blood, but against the rulers, against the authorities, against the powers of this dark world and against the spiritual forces of evil in the heavenly realms" (Ephesians 6:10-12).

10. Being a decisive person
    "Jesus replied, 'No one who puts a hand to the plough and looks back is fit for service in the kingdom of God" (Luke 9:62).

11. Growing in faith
    "Consequently, faith comes from hearing the message, and the message is heard through the word about Christ" (Romans 10:17).

12. Controlling their speech
    "Do not let any unwholesome talk come out of your mouths, but only what is helpful for building others up according to their needs, that it may benefit those who listen" (Ephesians 4:29).

13. Being wholehearted in their work
    "Whatever you do, work at it with all your heart, as working for the Lord, not for human masters, since you know that you will receive an inheritance from the Lord as a reward. It is the Lord Christ you are serving" (Colossians 3:23-24).

14. Maintaining pure thoughts

    "Finally, brothers and sisters, whatever is true, whatever is noble, whatever is right, whatever is pure, whatever is lovely, whatever is admirable – if anything is excellent or praiseworthy – think about such things" (Philippians 4:8).

15. Using their time wisely

    "Now listen, you who say, 'Today or tomorrow we will go to this or that city, spend a year there, carry on business and make money.' Why, you do not even know what will happen tomorrow. What is your life? You are a mist that appears for a little while and then vanishes. Instead, you ought to say, 'If it is the Lord's will, we will live and do this or that'" (James 4:13-15).

16. Being unselfish

    "Do nothing out of selfish ambition or vain conceit. Rather, in humility value others above yourselves, not looking to your own interests but each of you to the interests of the others" (Philippians 2:3-4).

17. Being a person of integrity

    "He has showed you, O mortal, what is good. And what does the Lord require of you? To act justly and to love mercy and to walk humbly with your God" (Micah 6:8).

18. Controlling anger

    "My dear brothers and sisters, take note of this: everyone should be quick to listen, slow to speak and slow to become angry, because human anger does not produce the righteousness that God desires" (James 1:19-20).

19. Overcoming bad habits

    "I can do all this through him who gives me strength" (Philippians 4:13).

20. Overcoming difficult temptations

    "No temptation has overtaken you except what is common to mankind. And God is faithful; he will not let you be tempted beyond what you can bear. But when you are tempted, he will also provide a way out so that you can endure it" (1 Corinthians 10:13).

STOP AND REFLECT:

What additional Scripture verses can you think of that could help believers in these areas of life?

_____

_____

_____

_____

_____

_____

_____

_____

_____

_____

_____

MAKING THE MOST OF EVERY OPPORTUNITY

Opportunities for discipling individuals are all around us, no matter where we live and work. We have learned over the years that there are plenty of young Christians who sincerely desire to be discipled by another Christian.

My wife, Jan, became a Christian as a young teenager, but no one discipled her in the basics of the Christian life. In university, Jan became friends with a Christian student, Dede. Dede invited Jan to join her Bible study. While studying 1 John 5:11-13, Jan found assurance of her salvation.

The next year, Dede and Jan became roommates. Dede taught Jan how to have a consistent time alone with God, how to give her personal testimony, how to witness to non-Christians, how to memorize Scripture verses, and how to lead a Bible study group.

Many years later, Jan reached out to women at a university in the city where she lived. She became friends with Fortunata, a student from Equatorial Guinea. Fortunata was from a Catholic background and had considered becoming a nun at one point in her life!

Jan invited Fortunata to study the Bible together, using the Bible study book called *Growing in Christ* and Fortunata's Catholic Bible. Fortunata came to understand for the first time that eternal life was a gift to be received by faith in Christ, not a

> **We make room in our lives for that which we truly value.**

reward to be earned. Fortunata chose to confess her need for Christ's forgiveness and to trust Christ alone for her salvation. She became a new creation in Christ!

While I (Mark) was teaching at a Bible college here in Kenya, I met a young man who was a relatively new believer. He was a physician at a nearby hospital. He accepted my invitation to read the Bible and pray together. Despite his busy schedule, he took time to prepare his answers to the study questions each week. Our friendship deepened as we shared our challenges, temptations, and prayer needs.

Many years have passed, and he has continued his medical practice and has become one of the leading surgeons in the country. But, more importantly, he continues to walk with the Lord and serve him faithfully. He is a loving husband and an excellent father for his children. I rejoice to see how the Lord has blessed and used him throughout his life.

Busyness and hectic schedules can present significant challenges in some situations. Timothy Ole Kileteny points this out when he writes:

> Discipling in the city can be challenging and frustrating. During my first three years of experience in these conditions I have found time and schedules very frustrating. I had previously discipled more than 15 people while in college. In Narok town of Kenya, I discipled two pastors, a businessman and one civil servant. In both cases we faced time constraints caused by different schedules, lack of time and hurried sessions.[85]

Such challenges can be overcome, but it takes a definite commitment by both the disciple maker and the one being discipled. If both of them consider this discipling relationship to be a priority in their lives, then they will find time to meet. In general, if we greatly value some activity, we will find time for it even it means sacrificing some other activities in our lives. We make room in our lives for that which we truly value and consider to be important to us.

DISCIPLESHIP ILLUSTRATED

One of the most effective tools we've found for helping people understand what spiritual mentoring and disciple making looks like is a DVD entitled *Walking with Jesus*. This DVD consists of five short (20-25 minute) episodes which show a pastor discipling two individuals (a village chief and a young man) who have become Christians. This video is not a lecture or sermon on how to disciple or mentor young believers. Rather it *shows* what disciple making, or spiritual mentoring, looks like.

The five topics covered in the episodes are "Assurance of Salvation", "Fellowship of Believers", "The Holy Spirit", "Walking in the Spirit", and "Growing in Christ". We highly recommend this DVD because we've found it to be extremely effective in helping others grow in their Christian life. All five episodes were filmed in Africa with local actors and actresses.

The best way use this video is to show one episode at a time. Then discuss together what can be learned from the pastor's example of discipling the two new believers.

HOW TO BECOME AN EFFECTIVE CHRISTIAN DISCIPLE MAKER

To become an effective disciple maker, make it a priority in your life to develop Christlikeness in your character. The individuals you disciple must see an example of godly living in your life.

Be intentional about developing your disciple-making skills through experience and training opportunities. Read books about discipleship and disciple making. Readers are leaders. Attend discipleship training sessions when you have the opportunity.

Seek to discover and use the spiritual gifts which God has given you. Every one of us who knows the Lord has at least one spiritual gift which has been entrusted to us to use for his work and his glory.

Be diligent to develop your natural God-given abilities. God has put you together with a unique combination of spiritual gifts and natural abilities or talents. The abilities God has entrusted to you are to be used for his glory, not yours.

Finally, pray for God to bring teachable younger Christians into your life. Look for individuals who are hungry spiritually with a desire to grow as Christians. You can be sure that individuals like this are around us if we look for them. The opportunities are limitless.

STOP AND REFLECT:

Can you think of some young Christian that you know who needs to be discipled? When could you approach this person and ask if he or she would like to meet with you on a regular basis to study God's Word and pray for one another?

_____

_____

_____

_____

_____

_____

_____

_____

_____

10
Finishing the Task

One of the athletes competing at the 1968 Olympics in Mexico City was a runner named Stephen Akhwari from Tanzania. He was competing with 74 world-class runners in the marathon race. Near the halfway mark of the race, Akhwari had a bad fall which resulted in one of his legs being badly injured with a dislocated joint. After lying on the ground for a few minutes writhing in pain, he got back on his feet, bandaged up his wounded leg, and resumed running the race. Everyone watching was astonished!

Over an hour after the winner had crossed the finish line, the relatively few spectators who had remained in the stadium heard what had happened to Akhwari and that he was still running! Finally, Akhwari entered the stadium running at a slow but steady pace. Every step he took made him wince because of his bloody and bandaged leg. The crowd began to clap and cheer him on. As he turned the final curve on the track, the enthusiastic applause of the crowd grew even louder. Eventually Akhwari was able to hobble across the finish line. The spectators were amazed by his endurance and determination to finish the race.

When members of the press interviewed him after the race, they asked why he had continued running the race even though he was injured and knew he couldn't possibly win the race. Akhwari's response was, "I don't think you understand. My country did not send me 7,000 miles to *start* the race. They sent me 7,000 miles to *finish* the race."[86]

STOP AND REFLECT:

What impresses you about the marathon runner's performance and his character? What can we learn from his example?

_____

_____

_____

_____

_____

_____

_____

_____

_____

Akhwari's performance shows us that it takes commitment and perseverance to finish a marathon. In a similar way, the Christian life can be viewed as a long-distance journey that requires a marathon mindset. The writer of Hebrews exhorts us to "run with perseverance the race marked out for us" (Hebrews 12:1). The race we are to run is one in which we follow Jesus's example and make disciples wherever he leads us. We enter the race when we put our faith in Jesus Christ and make a genuine commitment to follow him wholeheartedly. The finish line of the race is when our physical life ends and the Lord takes us home. God is looking for individuals who will not only start the race well but finish it well. He is looking for men and women who are committed to finishing the task he has given them.

In this book, we have challenged you to be a disciple who makes disciples. This is how you can leave a spiritual legacy. And this is how you can invest your life in things of eternal value. The authors of the *Africa Study Bible* emphasize this point when they write:

We make disciples by bringing people to Jesus, getting them to focus on him, and helping them to experience his grace and forgiveness. When we exhibit the characteristics of disciple-makers, and when we have counted the cost which through love we have decided to pay, the benefits are eternal.

Through the power of the Holy Spirit, the fruit we bear by making disciples will also bear fruit and those people will also go on to bear fruit and so on. Through this "fruit bearing," the gospel message will pervade the whole world.

Africans desire to leave a legacy. They want to be remembered for something they did long after they have departed this life. We will transmit the legacy of the Christian faith through discipleship (2 Timothy 2:2).

Many of us think eternal life happens in the future. The truth is that our new lives start with being called to be disciples of Jesus, and that calling lasts into eternity. Disciple-makers are those who have started their journeys towards eternity by living new lives right now and are calling others to join them.[87]

There is a proverb which says, "One cannot teach someone something has not seen or experienced oneself." In other words, we cannot expect to be able to make disciples unless we ourselves are truly disciples. As we come to the end of this book, we want to encourage you to fully commit yourself to this exciting and challenging task of obeying the Great Commission that Jesus gave to his disciples and to us as Christians today. There are several things you can do that will help you as you pursue this important task.

Be committed to studying God's Word, applying it to your life, and then teaching it to others. Ezra gave us a good example of what this commitment looks like: "For Ezra had devoted himself to the study and observance of the Law of the Lord, and to teaching its decrees and laws in Israel" (Ezra 7:10). We must apply what we learn before we attempt to teach others to do it.

It is important to show that you are making progress in your spiritual life. Paul stressed this point when he exhorted Timothy to "be diligent in these matters; give yourself wholly to them, so that everyone may see your progress" (1 Timothy 4:15). None of us have arrived spiritually. We are all under construction by the Holy Spirit. Those we are seeking to disciple need to see that we, too, are on the same spiritual pilgrimage even though we sometimes stumble and struggle along the way.

Watch your actions and your beliefs closely. How you live and what you believe are critical to being an effective disciple maker. Paul emphasized this when he wrote to Timothy, "Watch your life and doctrine closely. Persevere in them, because if you do, you will save both yourself and your hearers" (1 Timothy 4:16).

Work with individuals who are FAST: Faithful, Available, Sincere, and Teachable. Choose those who are faithful and dependable in their commitments and assignments. They need to be available to meet for training on a regular basis, have a sincere and genuine desire to be discipled, and have a teachable attitude with a willingness to learn from others.

Be patient with those you are discipling. Sometimes the individuals we are endeavouring to disciple may falter or fail when following through on commitments. We need to show patience with them. Remember, God and others have been very patient with us!

Keep in mind that it is God who makes spiritual growth possible. It is not through our efforts, but rather it is God who works in the hearts of those we are endeavouring to disciple. We have an important part to play as disciple makers, but ultimately it is God who transforms the lives of those we are seeking to disciple. Paul emphasized this truth when he wrote to the Corinthians, "I planted the seed, Apollos watered it, but God has been making it grow. So neither the one who plants nor the one who waters is anything, but only God, who makes things grow" (1 Corinthians 3:6-7).

Remember that your labour in the Lord is never in useless. Paul made this abundantly clear in his first letter to the Corinthian believers when he gave them this challenge: "Therefore, my dear brothers and sisters, stand firm. Let nothing move you. Always give yourselves fully to the work of the Lord, because you know that your labour in the Lord is not in vain" (1 Corinthians 15:58). Much of what we do with our lives is in vain, but what we do in terms of disciple making will never be in vain.

Invest your life in the lives of others spiritually. This way you are investing your life in things of eternal value. The only things that will last forever are God himself, his Word, and the souls of people. Seek to live a life of significance not merely a life of success. Success in the eyes of the world is measured by acquiring positions, power, and possessions. But a life of significance is one in which a person makes a lasting impact upon those around him or her. What kind of spiritual legacy do you want to leave behind?

Therefore, begin now, not later! It is easy to put off getting involved in discipling others until later in life when we think we will have more time to devote to this. Get involved right now wherever you are. Pray that God will bring you into contact with individuals who are eager to be discipled. Open your eyes. There are eager people around us, we just need to look for them.

The Great Commission applies to all of us who are disciples of Jesus no matter where we live or what occupation we have. It is not The Great Suggestion. And it certainly should not be The Great Omission. Each of us is called to be a disciple maker. We can all be disciples who make disciples and thus do our part in helping to fulfil the Great Commission that we've been given.

But where do you start? We suggest that you begin by praying and looking for one individual that God will bring into your life that you can begin discipling. It might be someone you lead to Christ. Or it might be someone who is already a Christian but hasn't had anyone willing to take the time and effort to disciple him or her.

In order to illustrate what disciple making looks like in real life, let me (Mark) share a personal illustration from my own experience. This illustration shows how all three methods of disciple making (congregational, small group, and individual) can work together concurrently.

Wani was a quiet but conscientious student who sat in the second row in my geography class at a senior secondary school in South Sudan. I was a member of a Christian rehabilitation organization serving there and had been assigned by the Ministry of Education to teach in this government high school. Since all the schools in Southern Sudan had been closed for five years because of the civil war, nearly all of the students in high schools in the late 1970s were in their twenties. Wani was in his mid-twenties as a form four (senior) student in the high school. I was only 26 years old myself, so some of my students were older than I was!

> **Seek to live a life of significance not merely a life of success.**

The Lord seemed to put this student on my heart, and I began to pray regularly for him. I didn't know if he was already a Christian, but I prayed that God would prepare his heart to receive the gospel if he wasn't. One day, after my geography class, I asked Wani to come by my office when he was done with his classes for the day. Sure enough, late in the afternoon, he stopped by to see me. We discussed some things regarding geography and then our conversation gradually drifted to spiritual things. I asked him if I could draw an illustration that shows how the Bible defines what a real Christian is. Wani said he would like to see it.

At that point we moved outside my office and sat down together on the veranda of the office building. I proceeded to draw and explain the bridge illustration which I had learned from a Navigator friend of mine when I was a university student. I have found that using an illustration like this is very helpful because it so clearly shows how sin has separated people from God and how Jesus is the bridge to bring us to a right relationship with God.

When I completed drawing and explaining the illustration, I asked Wani what he thought of it and he said he'd never seen anything like it before. In fact, he said he wanted to "cross the bridge" and commit his life to Christ! It was a thrilling moment for me when we prayed together, and I heard him ask Christ to come into his life to make him a new creation! It was my first time in Sudan to witness the birth of a new Christian. But it was just the beginning of my relationship with Wani.

Soon after his conversion, I invited Wani to join a small group of high school students who came to my house for a weekly Bible study which was held in the afternoon after classes were done. He became one of the most regular members of the Bible study group, growing spiritually by leaps and bounds. Every week, he came with his assignment completed. We used some Navigator Bible study materials that I had found to be quite helpful for young Christians. Wani also began regularly attending a local church where he was able to fellowship with other Christians and receive good biblical teaching from the pastor's sermons.

Wani continued to grow spiritually as he learned how to read and study his Bible, how to memorize Scripture, how to share his testimony, how to witness to his non-Christian friends, and other basic aspects of the Christian life. In addition to the weekly Bible study meetings, I would regularly meet with him to share and pray together. I was endeavouring to disciple him and help him grow toward spiritual maturity. These meetings continued over the next several months. By the time my term of service ended in Sudan and I left to return home to the United States, Wani had matured into a disciple-making Christian. Now it was his turn to invest his life in helping his fellow Sudanese in their walk with God.

I never had the opportunity to return to the Sudan to visit Wani, but I did have the privilege of meeting him in Nairobi about 20 years after I left Sudan. He was there taking a computer course. I was thrilled to see him again and to hear how the Lord had been using him to help others grow spiritually. He had become an editor of a Christian publishing company in Sudan and a lay pastor in a local church. God has used Wani in ways that I never dreamed possible.

Regardless of what occupation we might have, we can all be involved in investing our lives in the lives of individuals that God brings across our path. When I first met Wani, I had no idea of how God would use him in the future. God was already working in his heart, and my part was to befriend him, share the Good News with him, and disciple him as a new believer. In a way, I was like a Paul investing my life spiritually in the life of a Timothy.[88]

STOP AND REFLECT:

Can you see how all three methods of disciple making (congregational, small group, and individual) combined to help Wani come to Christ and to grow as a disciple? How did each of the methods contribute to Wani's spiritual growth?

_____

_____

_____

_____

_____

_____

_____

_____

_____

Our final challenge to you as fellow Christians is to persevere in following Jesus and making disciples. Never give up. Never turn back. Determine to not allow trivial pursuits to distract you from the mission God has given you. Sometimes, becoming busy with lots of good things can hinder us from being involved in the most important things. Let's keep focused on the task God has left us here to accomplish. Our mission is clear: to make disciples of all nations. We can do this with the Lord's help as we make disciples, one at a time. We need to take the Great Commission seriously. Let's determine to finish well so that, when the Lord calls us home, he will say to us, "Well done, good and faithful servant!"

STOP AND REFLECT:

What are some of the good things which we might become involved in that could potentially hinder us from pursuing the most important things?

_____

_____

_____

_____

_____

_____

_____

_____

_____

_____

STOP AND REFLECT:

How has reading this book affected your understanding of what it means to be a disciple who makes disciples? In light of these new insights, what are some specific applications you can make to your life as you move forward in your walk with Christ?

_____

_____

_____

_____

_____

_____

_____

_____

_____

_____

Z. Finish the task

You finished the task of reading this book! Now it's time to begin the task Jesus gave us. Would you pray this prayer with us to close our time together?

> Lord, we've been reminded of the commission you have given us to make disciples of all nations. Without a doubt, this truly is the most exciting, urgent, and important task in all the world. Thank you for allowing us this opportunity to make a lasting spiritual impact upon our world. Our time here on earth is brief, but it can be significant if we remain fully committed to this mission you have given to us. Help us to not be distracted by trivial pursuits which will surely take our focus off what you want us to be doing during our lifetime. Use us as your servants to advance your kingdom here on earth. We want to give our lives to things of eternal value. Amen.

May God bless you and keep you as you go out and make disciples.

From *The Discipler's Toolkit* | © Mark A. Olander | Published by Oasis International Ltd.

About the Authors

George Mutuku, Ruth, and their three children reside in Nairobi, Kenya. George earned his PhD in Biblical Studies at Africa International University. He is the Director of the Disciple Making in Africa Initiative. George also serves as the pastor of Christian ministries at the Africa Inland Church Ngong Road in Nairobi and he is a part-time lecturer at Africa International University.

Mark Olander and Jan have two adult children. They came to Kenya in 1984. Mark earned his PhD in Educational Studies at Trinity International University. He has taught at Scott Christian University, Moffat Bible College, Columbia International University, and Africa International University, where he is currently an adjunct faculty member in the Education Department.

Acknowledgements

We are indebted to several individuals whom God has used in our lives to disciple us and help us grow as Christians. We have personally experienced the benefits of being discipled by older and more mature Christians along the path of our lives. We are greatly indebted to those individuals who have poured their lives into ours.

We also want to recognize and thank our wives, Ruth and Jan, for encouraging us along the way to walk with the Lord and to give our lives to things of eternal value. In unique and powerful ways, they have influenced our lives and helped us to grow spiritually.

We are especially grateful to our colleague Randy Carpenter who spent a considerable amount of time doing the initial proofreading of the manuscript. His conscientious work has greatly improved the quality of this book.

Also, we want to recognize and appreciate the extremely helpful editing work done by Hannah Rasmussen and Laura Livingston at Oasis International Ltd. Their constructive criticism of the early revisions of the manuscript has provided us with numerous recommendations and ideas that have made the book much more readable and useful.

Furthermore, we want to thank our local church members and our students at Scott Christian University, Moffat Bible College, and Africa International University in Kenya who provided helpful insights while we studied disciple making together in a variety of settings.

The Bondei people of Tanzania have a saying, *Muungu akakwenka wegazi akwenka na ngata ya kwetwikia*, which means "If God gives you something to do, he will also give you the means to do it."[89] We believe he has given us the task of writing this book on disciple making and we have experienced his guidance, strength, and encouragement all along the way. In numerous ways he has given us the means to accomplish the task. To God be the glory, great things he has done! We pray that God will use this book to impact the church in Africa and move his kingdom forward.

This book began as an expanded version of the Teacher's Manual of the *Disciple Making in the African Church* materials (published by Loyal Communications). There is also a student workbook of the material, designed for use together in Bible schools or local churches. It is also available in Swahili (*Kufuasa Katika Kanisa la Afrika*) and French (*Faire des Disciples dans l'Église Africaine*).

Bibliography

In addition to the resources listed throughout the book, there are other Christian books, booklets, and journal articles dealing with the topics of discipleship and disciple making you may find helpful for further study:

Adeyemo, Tokunboh (ed.). *Africa Bible Commentary*. Nairobi, Kenya: WordAlive Publishers, 2006.

Adeyemo, Tokunboh. *Is Africa Cursed?* Nairobi, Kenya: WordAlive Publishers Limited, 1997.

Adeyemo, Tokunboh. *The Making of a Servant of God*. Kijabe, Kenya: Kijabe Printing Press, 1993.

Anderson, Keith R. and Randy D. Reese. *Spiritual Mentoring*. Downers Grove, IL: InterVarsity Press, 1999.

Bascom, Kay. *Hidden Triumph in Ethiopia*. Pasadena, CA: William Carey Library, 2001.

Bonhoeffer, Dietrich. *The Cost of Discipleship*. New York: Simon & Schuster, 1959.

Bruce, A. B. *The Training of the Twelve*. Grand Rapids, MI: Kregel Publications, 1971.

Coleman, Robert E. *The Master Plan of Evangelism*. Grand Rapids, MI: Revell, 1963.

Dais, Ron Lee. *Mentoring: The Strategy of the Master*. Nashville, TN: Thomas Nelson, 1991.

Downer, Phil. *Eternal Impact: Investing in the Lives of Others*. Signal Mountain, TN: Eternal Impact Publishing, 2005.

Eims, LeRoy. *The Lost Art of Disciple Making*. Grand Rapids, MI: Zondervan Publishing House, 1978.

Foster, Richard. *Celebration of Discipline*. San Francisco, CA: Harper & Row, 1988.

Hamlin, Judy. *The Small Group Leaders Training Course*. Colorado Springs, CO: NavPress, 1990.

Helm, David. *One to One Bible Reading*. Kingsford, Australia: Matthias Media, 2011.

Hendricks, Howard and William Hendricks. *As Iron Sharpens Iron*. Chicago, IL: Moody Press, 1995.

Hybels, Bill and Mark Mittelberg. *Becoming a Contagious Christian*. Grand Rapids, MI: Zondervan Publishing House, 1994.

Hull, Bill. *The Disciple-Making Pastor*. Old Tappan, NJ: Fleming H. Revell, 1988.

Hull, Bill. *The Complete Book of Discipleship*. Colorado Springs, CO: NavPress, 2006.

Janvier, George. *Being and Making Disciples: A West African Approach*. Nigeria. Great Commission Movement of Nigeria, 1993.

Janvier, George. *Discipleship: A West African Perspective*. Kaduna, Nigeria: Baraka Press and Publishers Ltd., 1993.

Jones, Bill. *Helping Others Believe in Jesus*. Columbia, SC: Crossover Communications International, 2004.

Jusu, John ed. *Africa Study Bible*. Wheaton, IL: Oasis International Ltd, 2016.

Kisulu, Peter Mualuko. *A Missionary Called Peter*. Kijabe, Kenya: Kesho Publications, 1983.

Kuhne, Gary W. *The Dynamics of Discipleship Training: Being and Producing Spiritual Leaders*. Grand Rapids, MI: Zondervan Publishing House, 1978.

Lingenfelter, Sherwood G. and Marvin K. Mayers. *Ministering Cross-Culturally: An Incarnational Model for Personal Relationships*. Grand Rapids, MI: Baker Book House, 1986.

Little, Paul with Scott Hotaling. *Certainty: Know Why You Believe*. Downers Grove, IL: InterVarsity Press, 1996.

McBirnie, William Steuart. *The Search for the Twelve Apostles*. Wheaton, IL: Tyndale House Publishers, 1973.

McClung, Floyd. *Basic Discipleship*. Downers Grove, IL: InterVarsity Press, 1988.

McQuilkin, Robertson. *The Great Omission: A Biblical Basis for World Evangelism*. Waynesboro, GA: Authentic Media, 2002.

Miller, Chuck. *The Spiritual Formation of Leaders: Integrating Spiritual Formation and Leadership Development*. Maitland, FL: Xulon Press, 2007.

Moore, Waylon B. *Multiplying Disciples: The New Testament Method for Church Growth*. Colorado Springs, CO: NavPress, 1981.

Morrison, Philip E. *The Multi-Church Pastor: A Manual for Training Leadership in a Multi-Church Setting*. Kijabe, Kenya: AIC Kijabe Printing Press, 2004.

Moyer, R. Larry. *Larry Moyer's How-To Book on Personal Evangelism*. Grand Rapids, MI: Kregel Publications, 1998.

Mtange, Nebert. "Discipling Nations: A Kenyan's Perspective." *Evangelical Missions Quarterly*, April 2010.

Musekura, Celestin and Faustin Ntamushobora. *Mentoring: A Remedy for the Leadership Crisis in Africa*. Nairobi, Kenya: Starbright Services Ltd., 2004.

Niemeyer, Larry. *Discipling: A Kingdom Necessity in the African City*. Nairobi, Kenya: Harvest Heralds, Inc., 1999.

Olander, Mark A. *Disciple Making in the African Church*. Nairobi, Kenya: Tropical Spring Media Kenya, 2013.

Olander, Mark A. *Improving Your Teaching Effectiveness*. Nairobi, Kenya: Print4All, 2019.

Olander, Mark A. "Tips on Testimonies". *Today in Africa*. Kijabe, Kenya: Kijabe Press, March 2005.

Osei-Mensah, Gottfried. *Wanted: Servant Leaders*. Ghana: Africa Christian Press, 1990.

Osei-Mensah, Gottfried. *The Making of a Servant of God*. Kijabe, Kenya: Kijabe Printing Press, 1993.

Petersen, Jim. *Evangelism as a Lifestyle: Reaching into Your World with the Gospel*. Colorado Springs, CO: Navpress, 1980.

Piper, John. *Amazing Grace in the Life of William Wilberforce*. Nottingham, England: Inter-Varsity Press, 2007.

Piper, John. *Don't Waste Your Life*. Wheaton, IL: Crossway Books, 2007.

Raman, Suraja. *Living and Witnessing: A Practical Guide for Leaders*. Singapore, 2017.

Raysbrook, Randy D. and Steve Walker. *One Verse Evangelism*. Colorado Springs, CO: NavPress, 2007.

Robertson, Roy. *The Timothy Principle: How to Disciple One-on-One*. Singapore: Nav Media Ltd, 2005.

Saint, Steve. *The Great Omission: Fulfilling Christ's Commission Completely*. Seattle, WA: YWAM Publishing, 2001.

Saunders, J. Oswald. *Spiritual Discipleship: Principles of Following Christ for Every Believer*. Chicago, IL: Moody Press, 1990.

Smith, Steve with Ying Kai. *T4T; A Discipleship Re-Revolution: The Story Behind the World's Fastest Growing Church Planting Movement and How it Can Happen in Your Community!* Bangalore, India: WIGTake Resources, 2011.

Stanley, Andy. *How Good Is Good Enough?* Portland, OR: Multnomah Books, 2003.

Stoddard, David A. *The Heart of Mentoring: Ten Proven Principles for Developing People to Their Fullest Potential*. Colorado Springs, CO: NavPress, 2003.

Sweeting, Donald W. and George Sweeting, *How to Finish the Christian Life*. Chicago, IL: Moody Publishers, 2012.

The Navigator Bible Studies Handbook. Colorado Springs, CO: NavPress, 1979.

Trotman, Dawson. *Born to Reproduce*. Colorado Springs, CO: NavPress, n.d.

Warren, Rick. *The Purpose Driven Life*. Grand Rapids, MI: Zondervan, 2002.

Wadge, Judy and Bob and Hope Carter. *Discipleship*. Kitwe, Zambia: Evangelical Church in Zambia, 2006.

Watson, David L. and Paul D. Watson. *Contagious Disciple Making: Leading Others on a Journey of Discovery*. Nashville, TN: Thomas Nelson, 2014.

Willard, Dallas. *The Spirit of the Disciplines: Understanding How God Changes Lives*. San Francisco, CA: Harper & Row Publishers, 1988.

Endnotes

1. Tokunboh Adeyemo, *Is Africa Cursed?* (Nairobi, Kenya: WordAlive Publishers Limited, 1997), 27-28.
2. John Jusu, ed., "The Great Commission," in the *Africa Study Bible*, (Wheaton, IL: Oasis International Limited, 2016), 1427.
3. Tom Nelson as quoted in Chris Adsit, "The Measure of a Ministry", *Missions Frontiers* (January-February 2011), 21.
4. George Janvier, *Discipleship: A West African Perspective* (Kaduna, Nigeria: Baraka Press and Publishers Ltd., 1993), 64.
5. Ibid., 11.
6. Jusu, ed., *Africa Study Bible*, 1427.
7. Joe Kapolyo, "Matthew," in the *Africa Bible Commentary*, ed. Tokunboh Adeyemo (Nairobi, Kenya: WordAlive Publishers, 2006), 1170.
8. Steve Smith with Ying Kai, *T4T: A Discipleship Re-revolution: The Story Behind the World's Fastest Growing Church Planting Movement and How it Can Happen in Your Community!* (Bangalore, India: WIGTake Resources, 2011), 35.
9. Adsit, 21.
10. Judy Wadge and Bob and Hope Carter, *Discipleship* (Kitwe, Zambia: Evangelical Church in Zambia, 2006), 5.
11. David L. Watson and Paul D. Watson, *Contagious Disciple Making: Leading Others on a Journey of Discovery* (Nashville, TN: Thomas Nelson, 2014).
12. Adeyemo, *Africa Bible Commentary*, 1223.
13. Dawson Trotman, *Born to Reproduce* (Colorado Springs, CO: Navpress, n.d.), 13-19.
14. Adeyemo, *Africa Bible Commentary*, 1223.
15. Kay Bascom, *Hidden Triumph in Ethiopia* (Pasadena, CA: William Carey Library, 2001), 64.
16. Belaynesh Dindamo, "Aledada, Astarke," in the *Dictionary of African Christian Biography*, 2004, https://dacb.org/stories/ethiopia/aledada-astarke/.
17. Helen Roseveare, *Living Sacrifice: Willing to be Whittled as an Arrow* (Fearn, UK: Christian Focus, 2007). Found via https://www.goodreads.com/quotes/697244-to-love-the-lord-my-god-with-all-my-soul.
18. Dietrich Bonhoeffer, *The Cost of Discipleship* (New York, NY: Simon & Schuster, 1959), 344.
19. Roy Robertson, *The Timothy Principle: How to Disciple One-on-One* (Singapore: Navmedia, 2005), 3.
20. Richard Foster, *Celebration of Discipline* (San Francisco, CA: Harper & Row, 1988).
21. Dallas Willard, *The Spirit of the Disciplines: Understanding How God Changes Lives* (San Francisco, CA: Harper & Row Publishers, 1988).
22. Francis A. Schaeffer, *The Mark of the Christian* (Downers Grove, IL, 1970), 35.
23. Bill Hull, *The Complete Book of Discipleship* (Colorado Spring, CO: NavPress, 2006), 150.
24. Gottfried Osei-Mensah, *Wanted: Servant Leaders* (Ghana: Africa Christian Press, 1990) 21.
25. Hull, *The Complete Book of Discipleship*, 148.

26. William Steuart McBirnie, *The Search for the Twelve Apostles* (Wheaton, IL: Tyndale House Publishers, 1973) 235-240.
27. Robert E. Coleman, *The Master Plan of Evangelism* (Grand Rapids, MI: Revell, 1963), 22-23.
28. Ibid., 31.
29. McBirnie, *The Search for the Twelve Apostles*, 45-75.
30. Ibid., 87-107.
31. Ibid., 108-121.
32. Ibid., 76-86.
33. Ibid., 122-129.
34. Ibid., 130-141.
35. Ibid., 174-182.
36. Ibid., 142-173.
37. Ibid., 183-194.
38. Ibid., 195-206.
39. Ibid., 207-234.
40. Bill Bright, "How to Introduce Others to Christ," https://www.cru.org/content/dam/cru/legacy/2012/03/How-to-Introduce-Others-to-Christ.pdf.
41. Comfort Arinlade Ayanrinola, "Ladeji ('Ladeji), Deborah Adeyemi," in the *Dictionary of African Christian Biography*, 2012, https://dacb.org/stories/nigeria/ladeji-deborah/.
42. Jim Petersen, *Evangelism as a Lifestyle: Reaching into Your World with the Gospel* (Colorado Springs, CO: Navpress, 1980).
43. Chuck Miller, *The Spiritual Formation of Leaders: Integrating Spiritual Formation and Leadership Development* (Maitland, FL: Xulon Press, 2007), 297.
44. Bill Hybels and Mark Mittelberg, *Becoming a Contagious Christian* (Grand Rapids, MI: Zondervan Publishing House, 1994), 40.
45. Bill Jones, *Helping Others Believe in Jesus* (Columbia, SC: Crossover Communications International, 2004).
46. Randy D. Raysbrook and Steve Walker, *One Verse Evangelism* (Colorado Springs, CO: NavPress, 2007).
47. R. Larry Moyer, *Larry Moyer's How-To Book on Personal Evangelism* (Grand Rapids, MI: Kregel Publications, 1998), 27-32.
48. Paul S. Dayhoff, "Zwane, Minaar and Grace," in the *Dictionary of African Christian Biography*, 2001, https://dacb.org/stories/southafrica/zwane-minaar-grace/.
49. Lois Semenye, "Christian Education in Africa," in the *Africa Bible Commentary*, ed. Tokunboh Adeyemo (Nairobi, Kenya: WordAlive Publishers, 2006), 1480.
50. A. B. Bruce, *The Training of the Twelve* (Grand Rapids, MI: Kregel Publications, 1971), 530.
51. *The Navigator Bible Studies Handbook* (Colorado Springs, CO: NavPress, 1979).
52. Trotman, *Born to Reproduce*, 17-18.
53. Mark A. Olander, *Disciple Making in the African Church* (Nairobi, Kenya: Tropical Springs Media Kenya, 2013), 22.
54. Jusu, ed., *Africa Study Bible*, 1427.
55. Rick Warren, *The Purpose Driven Life*, (Grand Rapids, MI: Zondervan, 2002), 236.
56. Ibid.
57. Ibid., 237-248.

58. Peter Mualuko Kisulu, *A Missionary Called Peter* (Kijabe, Kenya: Kesho Publications, 1983), 1-8.
59. Ibid., 18.
60. Ibid., 26.
61. Jusu, ed., "Ubuntu," in the *Africa Study Bible*, 1895.
62. Mark A. Olander, "Tips on Testimonies," *Today in Africa* (Kijabe, Kenya: Kijabe Press, March 2005).
63. Wadge and Carter, *Discipleship*, 45-46.
64. LeRoy Eims, *The Lost Art of Disciple Making* (Grand Rapids, MI: Zondervan Publishing House, 1978), 45-46.
65. Nebert Mtange, "Discipling Nations: A Kenyan's Perspective," *Evangelical Missions Quarterly* (April 2010), 212.
66. Joyce Landorf Heatherley, *Balcony People* (Georgetown, TX: Balcony Publishing, 2004).
67. Ron Lee Davis, *Mentoring: The Strategy of the Master* (Nashville, TN: Thomas Nelson, 1991).
68. John Maxwell, *Leadership Gold* (Nashville, TN: Thomas Nelson, 2008), 76.
69. Davis, *Mentoring*.
70. Warren, *The Purpose Driven Life*.
71. Regi Campbell, *Mentor Like Jesus* (Nashville, TN: B&H Publishing Group, 2009).
72. Judy Hamlin, *The Small Group Leaders Training Course* (Colorado Springs, CO: NavPress, 1990).
73. Ibid.
74. Ibid.
75. Smith and Kai, *T4T: A Discipleship Re-revolution*, 233.
76. Ibid.
77. "Home," Discovery Bible Study, accessed June 29, 2021, https://www.dbsguide.org.
78. Ibid., 234.
79. David A. Stoddard, *The Heart of Mentoring: Ten Proven Principles for Developing People to their Fullest Potential* (Colorado Springs, CO: NavPress, 2003).
80. Bolaji Yetunde Olaomo, "Agbebi, Adeline Adeotan Sikuade," in the *Dictionary of African Christian Biography*, 20114, https://dacb.org/stories/nigeria/agbebi-adeline/.
81. Floyd McClung, "The Measure of a Ministry," *Missions Frontiers* (September-October 2011), 20.
82. Semenye, "Christian Education in Africa," in the *Africa Bible Commentary*, 1480.
83. Keith R. Anderson and Randy D. Reese, *Spiritual Mentoring* (Downers Grove, IL: InterVarsity Press, 1999), 62.
84. African proverbs as cited by Laura Livingston.
85. Timothy Ole Kileteny in Larry L. Niemeyer, *Discipling: A Kingdom Necessity in the African City* (Nairobi: Harvest Heralds Inc., 1999), 48.
86. Donald W. Sweeting and George Sweeting, *How to Finish the Christian Life* (Chicago, IL: Moody Publishers, 2012), 17-18.
87. Jusu, ed., "Discipleship," in the *Africa Study Bible*, 1526-1527.
88. Olander, *Disciple Making*, 38-39.
89. Jusu, ed., "God Always Gives a Helping Hand to His Servants", *Africa Study Bible*, 1621.

OASIS INTERNATIONAL

Satisfying Africa's Thirst for God's Word

Our mission is to grow discipleship through publishing African voices.
Go to oasisinternationalpublishing.com to learn more.

INFLUENCE: LEADING WITHOUT POSITION
Philip E. Morrison & Hankuri Tawus Gaya
Do you have ideas for how to change your community, church, or nation – but feel powerless to make them happen? This book tells you how you can influence others to take action and start change, just as young men and women in the Bible did.

HIGHLY FAVOURED: OUR POWERFUL GOD'S COVENANT WITH YOU
Stuart J. Foster
The God of the Bible is not unreliable or inaccessible like the spiritual beings in African traditional religions. He chooses to have a covenant relationship with his people and we do not have to earn God's favour.

THE SISTERHOOD SECRET
Levina Mulandi
In this book, Dr Mulandi shows how discipling is more than Bible study or a church program. She shares how she empowers any woman to mentor younger women, guiding them to understand their identity, discern the purpose of their lives, and be transformed to be more like Christ.

BAESICS
Ernest Wamboye with Waturi Wamboye
In *Baesics*, Ernest and Waturi Wamboye give no-nonsense advice on how to build a fulfilling love life and marriage. Young adults in African cities feel marriage is priority but are often unprepared. Baesics addresses the relationship dilemmas many young adults are facing today from a Christian point of view.

THE DIVORCE DILEMMA
Ron Misiko & Ray Motsi
The authors share their experiences as pastors and as married people, as well as their areas of expertise in the legal system and Bible scholarship. From their different African contexts, they explain how to navigate the challenges we face today with biblical and practical solutions for divorce care in African churches.

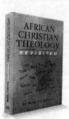

AFRICAN CHRISTIAN THEOLOGY REVISITED
Richard J. Gehman
For all African Christians, *African Christian Theology Revisited* is a powerful plea to think through your faith in African contexts under the authority of the Word of God.

AFRICANS AND AFRICA IN THE BIBLE
Tim Welch
This book shows the presence and the participation of Africans in the biblical text, helping demonstrate that Christianity is not a "white man's religion" and that Christianity has deep roots in African soil.

ANSWERS FOR YOUR MARRIAGE
Bruce and Carol Britten
Offers practical insights to marriage issues and facts on sex, pregnancy, child-raising, money issues, adultery, HIV, and sex-related diseases. If your marriage is in despair, look to this book for some answers for your marriage.

PARENTING WITH PURPOSE & AFRICAN WISDOM
Gladys K. Mwiti
This practical guide for Christians is a relevant, thoughtful presentation on the characteristics of parenting that delivers results.

A WITNESS FOREVER
Michael Cassidy
Michael Cassidy reveals for the first time what went on behind the scenes, away from the dramatic headlines, as South Africa inched its way towards the momentous election. Learn the first-hand account of the miracles that led to a peaceful end of apartheid in South Africa.

OASIS INTERNATIONAL PUBLISHING

oasisinternationalpublishing.com | oasisinternational.com

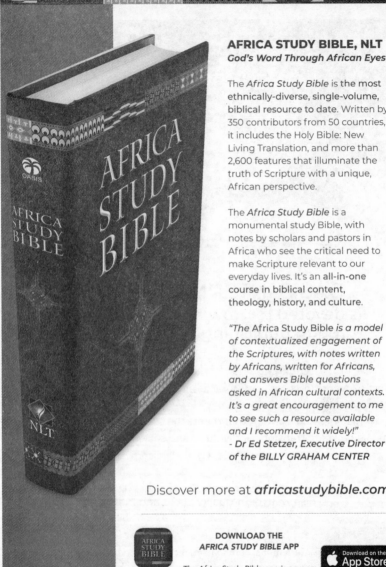